Sharon,

If life
was a house...
I'd List it,
Leverage it,
Buy it,
Rent it,
Then sell it
For a profit.
:)

John Bertler

8/26/08

THE STARE

By

JOHN BUTLER

*A True Story of
Death, Drugs & Destiny*

Copyright © 2007 by John Butler

ISBN 0-7414-4165-9

Published by:

PUBLISHING.COM

1094 New DeHaven Street, Suite 100
West Conshohocken, PA 19428-2713
Info@buybooksontheweb.com
www.buybooksontheweb.com
Toll-free (877) BUY BOOK
Local Phone (610) 941-9999
Fax (610) 941-9959

Printed in the United States of America

Printed on Recycled Paper

Published September 2007

This book is dedicated to my mom...

Who taught me to laugh at life,
When nobody else thinks it is funny.

And to my beautiful wife, son, friends and family...
Thanks for putting up with me.

Editor's Note...This book was written over a period of six years at different points in the writer's young and evolving writing career. This is a true story, however, some names and situations have been altered to protect the privacy of those involved and some creative liberties were taken for the sake of story telling.

CHAPTER
ONE

(John Butler #835, Lake Elsinore MX Track, AMA Championship)
"I just wanna go home..."

With numb hands, I shut off my motorcycle. A January sunset projected long shadows across the Mesa Marin foothills. My friend Jared's dirt bike growled to a stop as he parked alongside of me and quietly enjoyed the peaceful panoramic view of our youth. A cloud of dust settled over the track we had just ridden and the silence from our ceased motors saturated the shadows of the valley.

"It's cold," Jared uttered to himself, his breath like vapors. I rested my elbows on the handlebars and took in a deep breath. To my right I could see a silhouette of purple mountains like a dark silent giant, to my left was an orange haze of peaceful peach clouds floating into the horizon.

Dirt bike tracks etched on the side of blonde bluffs resembled my life at fifteen. Life was always a race...a race that I could win. Riding my dirt bike in the golden hills of east Bakersfield gave me fulfillment and further prepared me for my life to come. Within a few short years, I could be on the verge of the professional racing circuit. Life couldn't be much better for a sophomore in high school.

Jared looked at the watch mounted on his handlebars then looked at me with his dark eyes and asked, "What time do you have to be home?"

The sad shadow on the ground slid into the sands of time.

I searched for the shadows of the sun, yet found none, and answered, "My mom has another doctor's appointment at six o'clock. I have to be home to watch my sister…again."

"She has *another* doctor's appointment?" He asked with concern.

I **stare**d into the distant sunset, "Yeah."

He sat there quietly and fidgeted with his gloves. I could *feel* that he had something to say. With the gentleness of being a close friend he added, "She sure has been going to the doctor a lot lately, huh?"

My face-hardened and my chest became tight, "Yeah I know," I said sharply.

I looked at the setting sun and thought about the world on the other side of the earth. I wondered what other people saw as my sun was setting and theirs was rising. The contrast of life carried my thoughts away for a moment.

Jared's edgy voice cracked through my daze as he confronted me with a harsh reality, "You know your mom has a tumor, right?"

His mother must have told him what my mother had told her. My parents hadn't told me much about the doctor visits, perhaps not wanting to scare me.

My stomach dropped as my chest caved in. I sat up straight as Jared glared at me with uneasiness. The lump in my throat did jumping jacks as I muttered, "Yeah, I know," although I didn't know she had a tumor, or perhaps I was just denying that she seemed sick.

I looked down at my motorcycle and searched for truth. My man made machine remained the same; no answers came leaping forth. Jared sat there on his bike and waited for me to say something.

My heavy and disturbed eyes fell upon him, then to the ground.

Trying to change the subject he asked, "Do you want to ride some more before it gets dark?"

I nodded my head, although it was merely just a trained response. In unison, we slid our cold helmets over our heads and started our motors. The roar of my engine ripped through my body. He took off in front of me and the racing game of cat and mouse was on. Not wanting to think about my mother, I did my best to refocus.

With brute force our motors powered up the hill, made a hairpin turn at the top, then we descended downwards with full throttle. His rear tire pelted me with little rocks as my race bike raged closely behind his machine. The dust from his tires left a stream of dirt for me to follow; but I couldn't follow him, I had to win. An upcoming right hand corner was choppy with bumps and rocks, but if I could position my bike to the inside of Jared, I could rail right through to victory, thus winning the game.

With surgeon like precision, I guided my machine into a dark rut. Jared's motor popped with peak performance as he squared off the turn and ran directly into my route of attack. Our bikes collided and the pain of being run over consumed my body. He tumbled over his bike as I became trapped between both engines. His hot motor burned my leg. I squirmed around trying to dislodge myself.

"Sorry, dude, I didn't think you were that close," he apologized while trying to lift the motorcycles off me. I didn't really care. My mind was twisted about my mother and my body hurt. The harsh reality of life bit me in two. I sat there for a moment and tried to gather myself. Jared held up both bikes and waited for me to feel better.

"Are you gonna be okay?" He asked.

I heard him ask the question but my response was slow. My mind was somewhere else.

"Yeah, I'll be fine," I said as the sadness of my soul **stare**d at my shadow on the ground, "I just wanna go home."

CHAPTER TWO

"Dishes and all…"

Jared's green Ford Ranger backed into my driveway. Still in a quiet mood, I unloaded my dirt bike down a narrow steel ramp from his truck and into my garage. Jared drove away as I poked the small white garage door button. The mechanized roar of the massive aluminum door faded downwards as the spring-loaded doorway to the house stretched open.

I let the door slam.

Walking past my sister's room, I saw that she was playing with one of her nine-year-old friends. Danielle saw that I was limping and asked with a doll in hand, "Did you crash?"

With a brotherly glare I shot back, "Yeah."

She then pointed and teasingly laughed.

I walked into the kitchen and observed my mother preparing dinner for my sister and I. My defeated voice greeted her delicately, "Hi, mom."

"Hi, sweetie, did you have fun?" She asked while staring into the oven, her hand on the knob careful to adjust the temperature to perfection.

I didn't answer.

"Are you okay?" Her honest eyes hovered to my direction; the warm aroma from her baked goods filled my nostrils.

I responded bluntly, "Yeah."

"Did you crash?"

"Yeah," I said limping towards her.

She brushed my brown bangs to the side of my face, "Are you hurt?"

With a bratty voice and rolling eyes I fired back with "I'm fine, mom!"

She looked into me with her pale blue eyes and held my chin, "I need you to watch your sister, I have a doctor's appointment."

I rolled my eyes again and droned, "Yeah, I know Mom."

"What crawled up your butt and died?" She smarted sarcastically.

"No-th-ing." I answered with a tight throat trying to convince her as well as myself that nothing was bothering me; she may have believed me if my voice hadn't shuddered.

"John James," she exercised her motherly authority with the use of my middle name, her peering eyes searched for the root of the problem.

"I'm fine." I finalized with frustration.

Her eyes made one last probing inspection, then she returned her focus to the vegetables boiling over on the stove.

"I need you to set out the dishes for you and your sister please, then take out the trash," her loving voice was like a commanding general.

"Alright," my mouth muttered as I placed my tired hands on the thin white trash bag. My heart pounded with anxiety, wanting to know if she really had a tumor. I wasn't sure if Jared was right or if he was just assuming that she had a tumor. I didn't want to know. Or did I? The struggle of confusion and denial raged in my head.

With motherly instinct like a radar detector, my mom knew that something was bothering me. "John," she said almost as a whisper, "Are you okay?"

I paused, took a deep breath, then my words stumbled forth in pain, "Mom, do you have… a tumor?"

She straightened up with my directness and her face formed a solid façade as she searched for an answer. Silence seemed eternal.

"Well, honey," she too stumbled for the right words while wiping down the counter, "the doctors think that I might have a small tumor on my cervix; but I should be fine, don't worry."

Her comforting hand went to my shoulder, but I refused it. I was crushed. My heart exploded and my solid foundation was caving in; yet I withheld my tears. Crying wasn't for me. I was fifteen and "a brave man."

Wanting to escape the moment of pain and confrontation, I plucked the plump trash bag from the container and ventured to the garage, leaving my mother in the kitchen with an atmosphere of awkwardness.

My vision was somewhat dizzy as I threw the trash bag into the bigger trashcan outside. The darkness of the day had finally formed its black blanket in the sky above.

I **stare**d heavenward and searched for stars, but my search summoned a starless void. Nothing more than a deep breath could comfort me now.

A few minutes later I heard my parents coming through the garage as they prepared to leave for the doctor's office. My bearded stepfather Dave, emotionally strong and quiet, got into the driver's seat of the truck and told me to keep an eye on my sister.

I nodded.

My mother **stare**d at me from the passenger's seat, softly shutting her door, and waved with a reassuring, "I love you." Their vehicle rolled backward down the driveway, and then gracefully glided down the street.

Poking the garage door button once more, I headed into the house and saw that my mother had laid out a beautiful meal on the dark oak dinner table for my sister and me...*dishes and all.*

CHAPTER
THREE

"Drive straight sweetie…"

"Drive the speed limit, please." She said while pressing her foot to the passenger side floor.

"I am."

"The speed limit isn't eighty-five."

"Are you sure?"

"Sweetie, I've been driving this freeway a lot longer than you."

With my driver's permit tucked safely away in my wallet, I let my heavy foot off the accelerator in order to calm my mother's nerves. My mother had a habit of thinking that there was another brake pedal on her passenger side of the vehicle when I drove too fast.

"Slow down!" She would raise her voice while pressing her foot against the floorboard.

"Sorry," I'd say. Then my sister and I would chuckle.

Danielle's laughter filled the back seat, "You're driving mom crazy."

"Literally!" my mother added to the fun of the moment with a dramatic flare of her hands and a sarcastic smack to the back of my head.

"How many times do I have to tell you, mom? There isn't a brake pedal over there!"

My smile was wide and my joy was full. My mother gave me a playful punch to the arm.

"Maybe Dad could install one," Danielle chirped wittily.

"Oh, hush." She would say to settle the mother-children battle of sarcasm. Her blue eyes **stare**d us down. We laughed it off.

Dave had to work that day, so I assumed the responsibility of driving my mother to her radiation appointments in North Hollywood. It was the transition from spring to summer, when the snaking southbound traffic can witness colorful poppy flowers covering the green Grapevine valleys. It was a beautiful act of nature's transformation. Life and hope was possible.

The doctors my mother had visited through the winter and early spring had diagnosed her sickness as being a cervical tumor, yet they were confident that a round of radiation during the summer could cure the possibility of cancer. Doctors always had a way to cure everything, I thought, so I was optimistic that this minor problem in our lives would soon be gone. Within a few months, life would be back to normal. No more doctor's visits, no more driving to North Hollywood for radiation treatments, and no more pain.

Being fifteen with a driver's permit, I was excited to get the chance to drive my mom when Dave had to work.

The road became my escape.

I could focus straight ahead and see the great Grapevine Mountains off in the distance like a caravan of camels sleeping in the sand.

Sometimes the road would seem to be the only thing alive during the trip. I'd **stare** into the pavement and drive with purpose.

A few minutes down the road I glanced over at my mother and saw that the scenery behind her was a blur. Her head rested on a rose patterned pillow pressed against the window.

The drone of the drive had sung her heavy eyes to sleep. Although she was going to the doctor's office for radiation that day, she still took the time that morning to put her makeup on. A soft shade of blue eye shadow was like a blanket covering her eyelids.

I couldn't understand why she was sick, she looked healthy. In fact she was beautiful, an angel perhaps. The bumpy feeling of running over the white dots in the road rattled her awake.

"Drive straight sweetie," she said softly before slipping back into her slumber.

I refocused on driving. My young eyes **stare**d into the rear view mirror and saw a hazy Bakersfield being left behind. Hope was on the other side of the mountains. All I had to do was drive, wait in the boring doctor's office for my mom to be loaded up with radiation and then I'd drive her back.

It seemed simple enough…right?

CHAPTER
FOUR

(John, Danielle and Mom with a Siamese lamb at Ripley's Believe It or Not museum)

"Turning the page..."

"Hello," the receptionist said with a warm smile as she handed my mother a cold clipboard and pen.

"Hi," I said before grabbing the same People magazine that I had looked at the week before. Without much concern, Danielle and I went to our familiar seats in the waiting room-back in the corner, away from other people waiting for their loved ones. The pain of their faces was too much to understand.

By now, it was half way through summer, and the routine of delivering my mother for radiation treatments had soon become a way of life. Dave usually drove her down when he wasn't working, but as the demand for treatments soon became three times a week, he and I would take turns making the dreaded two-hour drive down south. The doctor's office was always the most dreaded place of boredom.

After signing in, my mother sat down with discomfort in a big cushy chair next to me. I turned the page to see the same picture as I saw the week before.

"It's hot," she said swiping the sweat from her upper lip. I turned the page to the same article that I had read last week, and gave my mother a distant nod. She took in a deep breath and looked around the sterile waiting room. Danielle colored in a coloring book. I turned the page.

"I'll be right back," she informed us as she stood up slowly. She then disappeared into the bathroom.

I turned yet another page, and somehow, had the sensation that I had seen it all before.

"Karen Donnelly, Karen Donnelly." A nurse's voice called out from an open door, which led to the radiation machine. I put my magazine down, motioned to the nurse that it would just be a minute, then I walked over to the bathroom door and gently tapped on it three times with my knuckle.

"Mom," my voice was soft. I could hear her vomiting, her painful lurching echoed through the door.

My voice became softer, "Mom, the doctor is ready to see you."

"I'll be right out, sweetie." A few more strained noises, then she came out. Beads of sweat lined her red face.

My soft brown eyes made contact with the pain in her blue eyes briefly, then they shifted back to my desired destination-my cushy chair of comfort located in the corner of the room-away from everybody else.

I picked up my People magazine and tried to motivate myself to reread another article about Bill Clinton.

While hiding behind the cover with *The Fifty Most Beautiful People* on it, I lifted my eyes to see my mother's weak body walking painfully towards the smiling nurse, "Hi there, Karen. Right this way," the nurse beamed.

As always, my mother was able to muster up a smile in return and sometimes a sarcastic remark, "Well…so much for digesting lunch." She'd say.

She and the nurse would share a laugh as they disappeared behind the door. As always, I tried to lose myself within the familiar pages of the magazine, hoping that I could find my sense of humor, my failing sense of happiness. So I did what I had done so many times before…

I turned another page.

CHAPTER
FIVE

"Hot and Hateful Summer Sun…"

A shiny diesel truck passed our white vehicle on the left side
as I drove back to Bakersfield for the last time that summer
beneath the angry August sun; the end of the season was
near, the weekly treatments in North Hollywood were almost
over.

They had failed.

Not only was it a cervical tumor, but the doctors had
now declared it as Stage Four cervical cancer. The worst
you could possibly have. The horizon of hope was becoming
hazy and distant.

I looked at our reflection in the polished aluminum
truck roaring by, my face lost amongst its mirrored
appearance. The gray road ahead of me no longer meant
hope, but despair. My mother slept in the passenger seat, her
head pushed painfully against a pillow. Looking in the rear

view mirror, I could see my sister taking a nap as well. My tired eyes looked misplaced upon my youthful face.

The radio, turned low, was gently strumming the chords of Eric Clapton's classic song Tears in Heaven. Looking into the mirror, I couldn't help but watch the tears well up in my eyes; yet I refused to grant them permission to pass down my face as I wiped them away before they had a chance to escape. With both hands on the wheel, I **stare**d straight ahead with a scowl on my face. A cloud of smog floated above the valley, which I called my home, my place of return: Bakersfield.

As the freeway descended from the grapevine and into the valley, I saw that the green mountains that I had seen earlier that spring had been scorched to a blonde oblivion. The hot and hateful summer sun had singed all plant life making everything dead and dry. The hope of another spring would have to wait.

Throughout the drive, like the many drives before, I would **stare** at my mother as she slept in the passenger seat. Her healthy beauty had vanished.

The dark circles under her eyes were constant, just like her pain. She no longer took the time to put on her makeup; doing so would take all of her precious energy. Her fluffy brown hair was now smashed and matted, similar to my spirit. The clothes she had worn for the past year were becoming baggy; they no longer fit as she continued to lose weight. The magical radiation treatments that the doctors had suggested a few months earlier had done nothing but wither my mother away like a sunflower scorched by the summer sun.

I felt confused about the entire situation. Was she going to die? Was she going to live? If she died, could I go on living? She was my existence, my life. Everything in my life had revolved around her in some way. Could I really handle it if she died?

The pain of acknowledging the fact that she might not be there next year killed me inside. I began to shut down emotionally. The very essence of my existence was leaving me. The thought of being motherless was too painful, so rather than accept the possibility of her death, I began to deny everything.

Detaching myself with denial made things seem bearable. She wasn't sick and she wasn't going to die because my mother was Supermom and she was going to live forever. The drive of denial became my only comfort, a comfort that would soon crash.

CHAPTER
SIX

"Shadow on the sidewalk..."

Centennial High School buzzed with students on the first day of school. Groups of students stood next to lockers and gossiped about their summer vacation.

Some blonde bimbo told her fellow fish head friends, *"Oh my gosh, like me and Jessica went to the mall and bought so many clothes, but my mom was like, 'you shouldn't waste your money!' So I was like, 'Mom, it's my allowance and I can do whatever I want, I don't have to listen to you!'"*

I walked past them like a ghost holding my binder and book closely to my right hip. My ears heard their shallow drama, but my heart couldn't relate.

I entered my English class and took a seat in the back row, away from everybody else. A boring teacher with a monotone voice commanded us to take out a piece of paper for our first writing assignment.

"Alright, I want everybody to write a one page essay of your summer vacation," he said drier than dust.

How original I thought to myself.

But did he really want to know about *my* summer? Did he really want *me* to stand up in front of the class and read *my* report of *my* summer vacation? Perhaps I could tell him about driving my mother to North Hollywood for radiation treatments. Perhaps I could tell him and the class about watching *my* mother lose weight at a rapid pace. Maybe I could describe in detail about the sounds of *my* mother vomiting or the way she emptied her urine from a catheter. Or maybe, just maybe, I could tell them how I was watching *my* mother die. Yeah, maybe that is what I could write about *my* summer vacation.

Perhaps that would get me an A+, maybe even some sympathy like, "Ah, gee that's too bad," with a sympathetic pat on the back.

But I didn't.

Instead, I wrote a generic story about dirt bikes. Gee, how fun it was to ride a dirt bike when your mom was dying at home. Gee, how fun it was to be at school and look at all the students who had healthy mothers waiting for them to get home after school. Gee, how great it was to be me.

The first semester of my junior year in high school went by like a shadow on the sidewalk. Somehow, I maintained my 3.8 grade point average, but something was missing; something was shallow. I sat at my desk and absorbed the classroom activities, but really, I wasn't there. School had always been easy for me, so it was more of a cruise control mode. When I was at school, I put on the mask that got me through my day. I laughed at shallow jokes, I made small conversation; I did what I had to do to get by.

The vibrant enthusiasm that I had once carried through my freshman and sophomore year seemed to slip away like a slow volcanic eruption.

CHAPTER
SEVEN

(Aunt Patty with my mom Karen in the kitchen in her final month)
"Flashes of fear..."

A cold and foggy Bakersfield winter passed by in shades of gray. The fog around Bakersfield was like a curtain of despair. School slid along slowly as the footsteps of death overwhelmed my daily thoughts. My mother managed around the house, but everything became more of a chore than before, nothing was as normal.

Not only did I begin to distance myself from school, but I also began to distance myself from all that I loved; my mother included. The isolation of my inner soul was intense. I needed to talk to someone, but I couldn't. The words became trapped within the darkness of my soul. Who could I talk to about watching my mom die?

What would I say?

People would often tell me that they were there for me if I needed to "talk," but what words could I use that they could understand? It all seemed shallow and meaningless.

My cruise control in school began to crash as my grades dropped to C's and D's, the worse they had ever been. My mother was going slowly, but my mind was already gone. The shadow of my life wandered through school like a soul without a body.

The short days of winter became the wandering days of spring. February followed a jaded January. The month of March made itself miserable while the agonizing days of April approached. Mother's day made itself memorable in May; the last picture of my mother was taken that day. All the photos we take in life, and yet, we never know which one will be our last.

Mother's day also marked the final countdown. The final months had dissolved into the final weeks. The doctors had thrown in the towel of any medical hope. Modern medicine couldn't change the cancer. Radiation and Chemotherapy couldn't erase the emotional pain. Gloom penetrated my every thought.

In mid-May I pulled into the driveway of my house after another passive day at school. I walked into the house and called out for my mother to see if I could go riding with Jared.

No response came forth.

"Mom!" I shouted louder.

No response.

Danielle sat in the living room doing her homework in front of the television.

"Danielle, where's mom?"

"I think she's in the bathroom. She's not feeling good."

"She's never feeling good," I said cynically.

Danielle shrugged her shoulders; her eyes still glued to the television.

I went to my mom's room and noticed that the bathroom door was shut. "Mom," I called out.

No response.

I knocked on the door, "Mom are you in there?"

"What, honey?" Her voice seemed weaker than usual.

"Can I go riding with Jared?"

Nothing but silence.

I waited for a few seconds, then being an impatient sixteen-year-old, I asked again, "Well, can I?"

Her voice came back more painfully through the door this time as she ignored my question for permission, "Is dad home yet?"

I looked at the clock, "No, it's only 3:05, he should be home in a few minutes though, so can I?" I asked again, still oblivious to my mother's suffering.

"I need you to stay here today."

I let out a breath of frustration, "Fine."

"When dad gets home tell him to come here, please."

Still clueless and somewhat upset that I couldn't go riding, I walked out of her room and saw my step dad Dave walking through the garage. "Mom wants you," I said, "she's in the bathroom. She's not feeling good." His face became heavy with concern.

He went into their room and closed the door.

I went to the living room and stole the remote from my sister. "Hey, I was watching that!" She whined.

Being the big brother had its advantages, and stealing the remote was one of them. "Too bad," I smirked, flipping through the channels finding something that I wanted to watch.

Danielle looked at me hesitantly while twirling a pencil in her hand, "John, what's wrong with mom?"

I took a deep breath not knowing how to explain to her what I didn't know that well myself. I shrugged my shoulders, "She's sick."

She sat there quietly and **stare**d at her unfinished fifth grade homework. She looked at me vulnerably and asked, "Is she going to be okay?"

I shrugged my shoulders once more, "I don't know," I answered, this time a scowl of internal pain covered my face.

Danielle looked down at her homework again. I could tell that a lot was on her young mind. I **stare**d at her as she thought. A few more moments passed, then she looked up at me with watery blue eyes and a quivering lip, "John, is mom going to die?"

I froze.

'How do I answer a question like that?' I thought. I didn't want to think about it, let alone discuss it with my sister who I thought was too young to understand the reality of death.

Her expectant eyes hoped that I would tell her that everything was going to be okay, but I couldn't. I just shrugged my shoulders and with quiet frustration gasped, "I don't know."

As the intensity of the moment held the room in painful suspense, we heard a knock at the door. I got up and answered it, only to be shocked by two paramedics carrying a propped up stretcher, "We got a call from this address," the head medic told me. Instantly a mixture of confusion and fear punched the wind from out my lungs. I tried to answer him, but I couldn't speak.

Dave walked up behind my sister and I, his face just as lost and afraid as ours, "She's in the back room," he told the medics.

"Daddy, what's going on?" Danielle's panicked voice pleaded for an answer.

"It's okay, sweetie. Just go finish your homework, mommy is going to be fine, don't worry." Dave tried his best to hide the trembling in his voice. I stood there numb, watching the paramedics disappear into the hallway as if I were watching a movie.

Dave looked at me, the horror in his eyes, "John, watch your sister."

"What's wrong?" My voice found its way out of my mouth.

"Just watch your sister please." Dave followed the medics into the backroom, and he shut their door behind them. I **stare**d out my front door and saw a white and orange ambulance parked on the street. The strobe lights along the top flashed fear and confusion into my heart. Neighbors began standing around outside trying to see what the commotion was about.

A flood of fearful tears welled up in my eyes but I wiped them away before my sister could see.

"John, what's happening?" She asked, her tears flowing freely.

"I don't know. Just go finish your homework."

My head began to spin.

"I want to see mom," she begged.

"Danielle, just go sit down!" The panic in my voice was increasing with every word.

One of the concerned neighbors waved me outside and asked, "John, is everything okay?"

I tried to answer him, but I broke out in tears. In between sobs I kept saying, "I don't know…I don't know what's happening." He put his arms around me as I buried my head into his chest. Another neighbor hugged Danielle in between her tears and confusion.

A few minutes later the paramedics came out with my mom on the stretcher with Dave following closely behind them. She looked pale. I **stare**d at her through a blur of teardrops.

Danielle cried out, "Mommy!"

"I'm alright, sweetie." My mother said weakly.

Dave's bearded face was focused on the medic's every move. He looked at me briefly, the fear still stuck in his eyes, "John, watch your sister. I'll call you from the hospital."

I nodded.

The medics lifted my mother into the ambulance and shut the door. I **stare**d at her through the small windows; not knowing if that would be the last time that I would see her.

Dave jumped into the car and followed the ambulance down the street. I stood on the front lawn completely dazed. The consoling neighbor looked at me, "If you guys need anything just ask."

I nodded numbly.

Danielle went into the house; her tear stained face still panicked.

I followed her into the house, but instead of going to the living room, I went back to my mother's room where she had been. I opened up the bathroom door, and saw the white toilet seat covered in blood. The water inside the toilet was bloody like the floor that surrounded it. The smell of feces fouled the air. I had never seen anything like it, as if something were brutally slaughtered.

My mother was dying and it had all come to this...

The bathroom...
The blood...
The terror.

Please God...
Please God...
Please God...

Let me die.

Not wanting my sister to see the bloody bathroom, I shut the door and walked back into the living room to keep her company. She laid on the couch sobbing. I took a deep breath and sat next to her, placing my hand gently on her back.

"Why is this happening?" She asked between sobs.

My face-hardened once again with the inability to answer her question, "I don't know, Danielle. I just don't know." We then softly cried together into the night, both wanting and waiting for an answer to the same question.

CHAPTER
EIGHT

(Christmas 1984)

"I love you..."

"Your mom is okay," Dave's voice verbalized through the phone later that night.

"What happened?" I asked softly, not wanting to wake Danielle up as she slept on the couch.

Dave's voice paused, perhaps not knowing whether or not he should tell me. "The tumor tore through the wall of her uterus. There was some tearing in her female parts."

"Is she going to be okay?" I asked.

"Well, she lost a lot of blood. But the doctor said she should be okay. They're working on her right now. I'm going to come home in a little bit. Just try to get some sleep." He said, with a flustered sound in his voice.

"Alright," I said.

Hanging up the phone, I went into my room and tried to get some sleep. My restless mind kept replaying the scene over and over again, until the darkness of my room finally consumed me into a deep sleep.

I came home from school the next day and saw that my mother was home from the hospital. She lay in bed, still pale and weak from the painful trauma of the day before.

I entered her room softly and greeted her even softer, "Hi mom."

"Hi honey."

"Are you okay?" I asked.

"I'll be fine. I just had some tearing." My mother always had a way of downplaying the seriousness of what was going on, she didn't want her children to be scared, although not knowing scared us just as much, if not more.

Wanting to believe her I asked, "Are you sure?"

She lay there quietly for a moment and thought. She then smiled at me weakly and told me to sit next to her. I walked over to her bed timidly and sat down.

She placed her frail hand on my leg and looked into my fearful eyes, "Are you alright sweetie?"

I shrugged my shoulders as the pain in my chest returned and my throat became tight.

Her hand rubbed my leg as she **stare**d deep into my eyes; "I love you, John. You know that right?"

My hand came to hers as I said, "Yeah, I know mom, I love you too."

"I need you to be good," she told me.

I nodded in response.

"I'm so proud of you," she smiled. I tried to return the smile, but I just **stare**d at the floor beside her bed, the edges of my mouth holding back my pain.

"I don't want you to hurt," I said.

Her fingers caressed the top of my hand, "Don't worry about me. Just know how much I love you. You're my precious little boy."

The folds of my mouth lifted to a boyish smile.

"I love you too, mom. But-," I hesitated for a moment, "I don't want you to die."

She **stare**d at me as I **stare**d at her. "I know sweetie, but we all have to die sometime."

"It's not fair," I told her as the pain within my chest mounted even greater than before.

"I know. But you can't let that hold you back. I believe in you, John. You're going to do so much in life; you can't let this hold you back."

I glared at the floor again as her hand continued to comfort mine.

Dave entered the room with a blue bottle of morphine, "How are you doing honey?" He asked her.

She **stare**d at me for a second longer, then she looked at him and said, "It hurts a little, but I'm okay."

"The doctor said this should help with the pain," Dave said as he measured some liquid morphine into a small cup. He put it up to her lips and she swallowed it, wincing at the taste.

Dave looked at me, the pain in his face as evident as mine, "Your mom needs some rest."

Still holding her hand, I nodded in agreement.

"I love you mom."

"I love you too sweetie," she said, with our eyes still locked as I left the room.

CHAPTER
NINE

"Everything happens for a reason…"

The last days of May turned into the first few days of June. My mother drifted further and further away into a sea of morphine, a powerful opiate drug given by doctors to dying people in pain. The faint footsteps of death now sounded like a marching army. The local hospice provider brought my mom a medical bed for her bedroom, to give her added comfort in her final days. Dave's sister Patty, my aunt with a heart of gold, came up to help.

"How are you doing, John?" She asked.

I looked toward her with blankness at the question. She saw the look on my face and understood that I couldn't answer with words. Her love and compassion held me close with a hug.

"I just don't want her to suffer anymore," I told her.

"I know," she said softly, "I know."

Patty and Dave did their best to give my mother any comfort possible. The morphine distorted my mother's thoughts and speech. She was lost and dazed between the stages of life and death.

Patty would try to spoon feed her soup, but my mother pointed to the wall with a shaky hand as her leg flinched uncontrollably, "The dog. Look at the dog."

"Karen," Patty's voice tried calling into my mother's morphine delusion, "the dogs are right here next to you." My two dogs looked up at the bed; they too could sense that my mother was dying.

Patty tried putting the spoon to her mouth again, but my mother's hand pointed again to the images in her mind.

I stood in the doorway and watched this for a few minutes, and then I retreated to my room to be alone. It was the afternoon of June fourth and the shadows in my room were darker than normal.

I sat in the quietness of my room. Nothing made sense because nothing seemed to matter anymore. It was the final week of school and I had failed all of my classes. But it didn't matter, nothing did.

As my mother lay in the room down the hall and died physically, I stayed in my room and died emotionally. Crying no longer made sense, so I didn't even try. I just sat there looking into a mirror not wanting to be the person who **stare**d back at me.

The look on my face was deep and distant.

The shadows of my room grew into the darkness of the night, but the darkness didn't seem to matter either, I just continued to **stare** at the other person in the mirror.

A gentle knock came upon my door. Dave twisted the doorknob and pushed the door open, "John?"

I **stare**d at him; he **stare**d back at me.

His face was lost and full of pain.

"Yeah." I said without words.

He was just as emotionally shut down as I was. "You might want to spend some time with your mom," he looked at me, "you know…if there is anything you want to say, or anything…" he had a hard time speaking. But he didn't have to say anything; I knew what he meant.

I nodded and stood up. Walking down the hallway, I saw the TV projecting gray images in her darkened room. The walk seemed to take forever as if in slow motion.

Sitting down in the shadows beside her bed, I reached for her hand wanting to feel the comfort that I had always reached for as a child growing up. Instead, her hand jolted out of mine as she mumbled something through the morphine. Scared and alone without my mom to comfort me, I erupted into tears. All the crying that I had been bottling up now poured out violently.

"Mom," I cried with deep sobs, "Please don't leave me!"

Tears streamed down like raindrops from heaven.

I buried my face into my hands and wept louder each time. "Please don't leave me! I need you!" Her leg twitched as the gray TV flickered.

"Oh God! Please don't take my mom! Please don't take my mom away from me!"

My chest shuddered with every painful plea. It could have been minutes, although it seemed like hours, but I just wept and sobbed like I had never before.

My mother, hearing my cries, looked at me, "John," she said still shaking uncontrollably. She was struggling to fight through the morphine. I wiped my tears with my shirt and leaned in closer as she told me clearly, "I love you sweetie, you'll always be my little boy."

I squeezed her hand, "I love you too mom. I love you too."

She tried to smile but the morphine washed over her again, leaving her body to cringe uncontrollably. I couldn't stand the pain anymore; I had to get away, I had to escape. I stood up with blurry eyes and left the room, not realizing that that was the last thing she would ever say to me.

I walked out the door of the house and got into my truck to escape confronting the pain of death. Driving around in complete hysteria I began shouting and punching my steering wheel, "Why is this happening!" I pleaded, "Why are *You* doing this?"

The darkness of death surrounded my little truck as I drove up to the bluffs on the East Side of Bakersfield. I pulled over facing the West Side of Panorama drive, a night lit view of the city behind a blur of teardrops. Burying my head into my arms, I continued to let out deep sobs mixed with anger.

"God, why are *You* doing this to me!"

I punched the dashboard several times while shouting to the sky.

"Tell me! Why are *You* doing this!"

As those words escaped my mouth, a soothing calm came over my body. The sands of time seemed to stop as a voice as gentle as the wind went through my soul and said, "*Everything happens for a reason…Everything happens for a reason… Everything happens for a reason.*"

Smearing my tears into my sleeve, I **stare**d out at the view and saw the lights of the city shining like gold glitter on a black blanket. I repeated the phrase to myself, "*Everything happens for a reason…Everything happens for a reason…Everything happens for a reason.*" A peace beyond all human comprehension consumed my being.

I didn't fully understand what those words meant yet, but the peace given was what I needed to ease the pain. In my darkest and loneliest moment, God came to my comfort. I sat there and let the words saturate my heart, mind and soul. I had always believed in God, but I had never experienced Him in such a real way before that night.

As the heavy hand of agony eased, I looked out the darkness of my truck and saw the lights of the city sparkle. I knew in my heart that the time had come to say goodbye to my mom. I started my truck and drove back home.

As I pulled into the driveway, a sick feeling of death's shadow fell over me once again. I walked into the house and headed to my mother's room, but stopped short as I saw that she was sleeping. Not wanting to disturb her, I whispered, "Good night mom, I love you." I stood in her doorway and **stare**d at her for a second longer.

Her legged twitched, the gray TV flickered. Then I dropped my head and went to my room to go to sleep.

About five the next morning my door opened. Dave stepped into my room and tried to say something but he couldn't. He didn't have to; I knew by the look on his face what had happened. I got out of bed and followed him and Danielle to where my mom was.

A soft morning light filled my mom's room as an empty feeling filled my chest.

We turned the corner into her room and there she was.

Silent.

Still.

Staring into our suffering souls.

As Danielle saw our mother lying there motionless in bed with her head angled to the right staring out the sliding glass door, she exploded into tears. Dave held her tightly. I stood a few feet away, completely numb and distant, somewhat absent from my body.

Then I saw the **stare**. The glossy **stare** of death in my mother's blue eyes, the same blue eyes that I had seen all of my life as her little boy. It was a **stare** so deep, so peaceful, so distant. I began to wonder what she was looking at as she took her last few breaths. Perhaps she was staring at an angel who had arrived through the sliding glass door of our house to take her to the pearly white gates of heaven.

I knew that **stare** would be singed into my mind forever.

I was paralyzed with the presence of death.

After a few minutes, Dave and Danielle left the room sobbing. I continued to stand quietly staring back into my mother's eyes. She was no longer in pain, her struggle was over.

I remained numb for a few more moments and then I walked over to her bedside. Looking into her pale blue eyes one last time, I kissed her on her forehead and whispered, "I love you mom."

Then I closed her eyes for eternity and exited her room, entering into the hollowness of the hallway and into the shadows of my soul.

CHAPTER
TEN

(Mom's grave, Hillcrest Cemetery, Bakersfield, Ca)

"She is dead, and so am I…"

The memories in my mind suddenly become black and white at this point. I remember floating out of her room, as if I *was* a ghost. I was hollow. I was empty. I really wasn't there, in a sense; I died with my mother.

A grief counselor came to our house to help us deal with her death. Dave and Danielle tried their best to explain the pain that they felt, but I just sat there:

*N*umb.

*A*bsent.

*D*istant.

*A*lone.

"How are you handling your mother's death," the concerned counselor asked me.

The confusion of emotions and thoughts left me with a lack of words.

"I'm fine," I said falsely.

She looked at me, knowing that I wasn't "fine."

"Are you sure you're okay?" She sympathized.

I didn't want to talk to her or anyone else, I wanted my mother.

"Yeah, I'm fine," I told her once more, then I got up off the couch and left the room. She couldn't understand me, nobody could.

The days following my mother's death are blank. I don't remember what happened. The fleeting coattails of death have an ability to erase all memories. Death's sting had struck my heart, mind and soul. My world was shattered. Dave and Danielle retreated inwards, as well, but I can't remember that either.

None of us can.

We were numb and we were lost.

My mother was the shepherd of our lives, and now that she was gone, the flock was scattered.

The funeral was like a movie: There I was on a hot day in June, greeting people in a funeral parlor, my mother's body laying in a beautiful casket surrounded by flowers dimly lit from above, you know, to set the mood for mourning.

Can you see me in the movie?

Look. There I am.

I am the one smiling, shaking hands with people.

Do you see me?

I am walking around, laughing, and cracking jokes with family and friends. My mother is over there, do you see her?

There she is. She is the one lying down in the casket.
Asleep.

She's about to wake up. There she is.

Here I am, shaking your hand, smiling, laughing.

Denying.

I walked up to my mother's casket with my friend Jared. A denying voice raged within my head: *Look at her, her face so perfect, the make up done by angels. She is an angel. An angel that is asleep. She isn't dead. She is sleeping. Wake up mom, wake up!*

Jared put his arm around me thinking that I was about to burst into tears, but instead, I joke that he is trying to make a pass at me. He smirks half-heartedly and wipes the tears from his eyes, but why is he crying?

I'm not crying, look at me, I'm strong.

I don't cry.

Look at me, the sixteen-year-old superhero, the motherless boy that doesn't cry. Aren't you impressed by how strong I am?

Look, no tears.

Look mom, I'm not crying because I am strong, mom, go ahead, open your eyes, look at me mom!

People filed in one by one to pay respect to my mother. I continued to walk around in my own little world, completely oblivious to pain, to truth, to death.

My mom isn't dead. She is going to get out of the coffin any minute now and say, *"Tada!"*, like she was just performing a magic trick. She always had a sense of humor, and surely this was just some joke she was playing. She couldn't die. Aren't mothers immortal?

An internal dialogue of denial continued to block my emotions: *She can't die, she can't leave me. I'm her little boy. I need her. She loves me; she wouldn't leave me, no way, no how...*

Suddenly I am in a car following a hearse. There are cars following us. But why? Where are we going? What's going on? Where's my mom?

We walk onto a sprawling carpet of green grass with gray tombstones stitched across as far as my eyes can see. I see chairs, I see people. People wearing black, people crying. There I am, carrying the side of a casket looking straight ahead; looking for my mother.

She should be here too, I think to myself. But where is she?

I see myself looking at a box next to a hole. A beautiful bouquet of flowers decorates the top of it. I look to my left and see Dave and Danielle crying, but why? I look to my right and see family and friends crying, but why? I look straight ahead and see a box. What's in the box? What's going on? Where's my mom?

A preacher stands and speaks, but I can't hear him. I see his lips moving, but the words don't make sense. What is he saying? What are we doing?

After a few minutes, maybe hours, I don't know how long, perhaps an eternity, I find myself following my Dad to his car. I get in the back seat and shut the door. I see other people doing the same. Looking out across the grass I see workers lowering the casket down into the ground. They take a shovel and throw a pile of dirt on top of it, and then suddenly it hits me:

THEY ARE BURYING MY MOTHER BECAUSE MY MOTHER IS DEAD.

Truth has never been so cruel. I sat back in my seat and gasped realizing that it wasn't a movie…this was *my* life, that was *my* mother.

She is dead, and so am I.

CHAPTER
ELEVEN

(1998 Bakersfield Supercross where I won the 125 series)
"Chasing comets…"

I'm in a mall. I see people swarming around from this store to that. Lights are flashing, people are walking, talking, holding hands, laughing. There is no order there is just chaos.

Amongst this chaos, I see a little boy walking in front of me. He is lost. I walk up behind him, knowing somehow that he is lost. He is wandering around, searching, looking, crying. I know that he is lost. I walk up behind him and ask, "Are you lost little boy?"

He turns around with tear filled fearful eyes, and I see that his face is my face, and he cries out, "I lost my mommy!"

Then I scream.

I wake up panicked. The darkness of my room offers no consolation. Looking at the clock I see that it is 4:20 in the morning, and realize that it was just a dream. My life was a dream, a dream that I couldn't seem to wake up from.

The weeks following the funeral seemed fake. My life was fake. Nothing was real anymore. Nobody was real because I wasn't real. I tried to find truth, but truth couldn't be found, because I couldn't be found. I was lost.

Dave and I tried to regroup our lost passion for traveling to the races, but it was empty. We would see people at the races, people we hadn't seen in a long time, and they'd ask how my mother was doing.

I'd **stare** at them blankly and say; "She died."

Their faces would fall as their eyes searched for the right words to say to me, but they couldn't.

"I'm so sorry," they would all say.

'No you're not, but thanks anyway,' I wanted to say to them. But I didn't. I just nodded with false appreciation to their false concern. Everyone was fake, because life was fake. Nothing was real. Nothing mattered.

Instead of racing and exercising, I found myself hanging out with my friend Brady. I had been friends with Brady throughout my mother's sickness, but now his friendship had a valued perk: he liked to party, he liked to drink. I never drank before because I was a good kid from perfect suburbia, but now, life wasn't so perfect and drinking seemed to ease that lack of perfection.

The weeks of that summer stumbled by in a drunken blur. My seventeenth birthday went by virtually unnoticed. Dave and the rest of my family tried their best to give me a birthday party, but it was not the same. Nothing was.

Feeling lost and vulnerable, I started my senior year of high school. I see people, but people don't see me. I am invisible. I am nobody. I am nothing.

Though racing lost its appeal, I still went riding as much as I could.

There I am…do you see me?

I am jumping through the air, my bike launches into orbit, ten feet, twenty feet, a hundred feet, a thousand feet! Planes and birds are in danger, because I am flying, I am escaping. Look! Look at me jump, do you see me? There I am, jumping over mountains, flying over clouds, chasing comets. I can jump over the moon, if I want; I can leave this world behind and never come back. I am not of this world because I don't like this world. This world is fake. Then I land back into this earthly reality, just for a moment, and then I rev up my engine and try to do it again. Perhaps this time I will crash and I will die.

A guy I went riding with, a well to do businessman named Brett, sat on his tailgate one day and asked me about my life.

"What else do you like to do besides riding?"

I thought for a moment, the question bringing me down to reality. "Well, when my mom was alive, we had a motorcycle business called Factory Edge Accessories. We used to sell motorcycle parts at the racetracks. I like doing business stuff."

"Really?" He answered sounding intrigued.

"Yeah, I like marketing and advertising," I told him.

"Well, I'm looking to invest money into some sort of business, you think you would be interested in coming up with some ideas?"

"Sure. How much money are you thinking about investing?" I asked.

"I dunno, probably about twenty thousand," he said nonchalantly.

My eyes widened. Being seventeen I had never dealt with that much money before, and suddenly, the darkness of my world didn't seem so desolate.

I have a goal.
I have a focus.
I have a purpose:
Business.

CHAPTER
TWELVE

JOHN BUTLER
Owner
Marketing
Sales
Ph- / FAX 805-589-4881

"What's Dickweed?"

My mind began to spin together different opportunities, everything from a dirt bike shop, to motorcycle products, but as I tell my friend Brady about the idea, he suggested something different.

"Why don't you do Dickweed?" He said with a spark in his eye.

"Dickweed? What's that?"

Brady walked over to his closet and pulled out a shirt. He threw the shirt in my lap, and I held it up by the shoulders.

"Dickweed," I said with a chuckle. The word had been designed into a cool looking logo screen printed across the chest.

"Yeah, my parents and I started it when I used to race. I used to have a wiener dog named Sir Ruben Dickweed the 21st, and when we were thinking of a name for a T-shirt line, the dog walked through the living room. So we called it Dickweed," Brady said smiling. "We sold a bunch of shirts, but then we stopped. You should tell that Brett guy to invest in that, we could make bank."

My interest flared up. The grin on my face expanded as my mind raced with different possibilities. "Yeah, he could front us the money then you and I could sell the shirts, we'd be rich!" I said swept away with youthful ambition.

Brady fueled the fire even more, "Dude, we can get these printed cheap through my uncle because he has his own screen printer, then we could sell them for fifteen bucks a pop! If we sold a thousand of these, that'd be fifteen grand! We could be fifty-fifty partners and just pay Brett back with some interest."

My eyes widened. I went home that night and started making designs and marketing plans. The next day I called up Brett with excitement in my voice.

"Brett! I've got the perfect plan."

"Oh yeah, what's that?"

"My friend Brady had this clothing company called Dickweed," I said enthusiastically trying to pitch the idea.

Silence.

"What's it called?" He asked hesitantly.

"Dickweed Sportswear."

He hesitated again, "Hmm, I don't know about the name. What does it mean?"

I tried to explain to him that it wasn't as offensive as it sounded. I told him that it was named after a wiener dog, but after fifteen minutes of continued explanation and youthful reasoning, he said that he wasn't interested, partly because he was a father of four and didn't find it appropriate.

Bummed and crushed in spirit, I called Brady and told him that it was a no go.

"Why not?" He asked.

"He didn't like the name Dickweed."

"Bum deal," he said.

"Yeah. But I think we could sell a lot of these shirts, who else could we ask?"

"I don't know, what about your Dad?" He suggested.

I thought for a moment, then my step dad Dave walked through the kitchen.

"I'll call you back," I said hanging up.

"Hey Dave, would you be interested in loaning me some money to start a business?" I asked.

He looked doubtful for a moment, "What kind of business?"

I told him my plans, showed him my designs and suggested that it would be great business experience.

"I'll think about it," he said.

The next day I was in the kitchen and Dave came in, "Hey John, I was thinking about your shirt idea. How much do you think you would need?"

Excited and not wanting to ask for too much I said, "I don't know, maybe six hundred bucks or so."

"Alright, but I expect you to pay me back," he said sternly.

"I will, I'll even pay you back with interest," I said earnestly trying to close the deal.

"No, you don't have to do that. Just pay me back when you sell the shirts."

"Deal." I said with a huge grin and a handshake.

I called up Brady immediately, "Dude, guess what? Dave is going to give me six hundred bucks to get shirts printed!"

"No way," he said surprised. "Sweet."

My mother's death started becoming a distant memory, mostly because I didn't want to deal with it and now because I had something else to focus my mind on. Rather than deal with the painful emotions that lingered in the back of my mind, I just jumped headfirst into creating business plans and designs. Avoiding the pain was easier than dealing with it.

Halfway through September, Brady and I began to file papers for a fictitious business name and other documents so we could be a real business. The old lady at the county clerk's office looked at the two of us seventeen-year-olds above her thin wire glasses.

We smiled brightly.

She raised an eyebrow.

Perhaps she had never seen kids so ambitious, so eager to do business, or perhaps we had messed up on our application. Either way, we didn't care; we were becoming entrepreneurs, yes, we were heroes, our capes flapping in the wind, a huge red and yellow letter E stretched across our chest.

She looked at the clock, it was almost lunchtime, so she just stamped her approval and processed the applications. And our Dickweed journey had begun...

CHAPTER
THIRTEEN

"Wanna pet my wiener…"

A week later Brady and I drove to the coast and picked up the shirts from his uncle's screen printing business. I opened up the box of our first hundred shirts and smiled victoriously.

"Those are sweet," Brady grinned.

Putting on a shirt I said, "Dude, we're going to sell a ton of these!"

We drove back to Bakersfield and discussed our plan of executing the sales.

"I'll just be the cool guy," Brady said with a smirk. His job was to get people interested in the shirts and I'd do all the rest since I had former business experience doing marketing and sales for my parents' motorcycle accessory business.

The next day I went to my school with a box full of shirts in the backseat of my little truck. I walked into my first period economics class with a handful of shirts. I stood in front of the class and made my announcement, which sounded somewhat like a used car salesman crossed with a circus ring leader, *"Ladies and gentlemen, boys and girls of all ages! I am proud to present to you the newest clothing company to hit the high school scene…***Dickweed!**"

Silence mixed with smirks and raised eyebrows.

"Yes that's right ladies and gentlemen, you have the opportunity to buy the shirts first and direct from the source. Now, I know what you're thinking to yourself, 'Wow, I really want one of those shirts, how can I get one?' Well I'm glad you asked yourself that, because I'm gonna tell ya! For only fifteen dollars you can be one of the first people to be wearing this brand new Dickweed shirt! What you say? Only fifteen dollars? Yes that's right, only fifteen bucks!" I smiled brightly holding up a shirt while modeling the one that I was wearing.

My economics teacher, Mr. Wells, leaned against his desk with his arms folded and laughed.

"Dickweed, huh? What inspired this entrepreneurial endeavor?"

"Give me fifteen bucks and I'll tell you," I said with a salesman's charm.

He reached for his wallet and pulled out fifteen bucks, "I'm impressed, Mr. Butler, you're quite the salesman."

The rest of the class chuckled as I went around the room selling shirts. Everyone asked what Dickweed meant, and they were all surprised to hear that it was named after a wiener dog.

In between classes, I ran into Mr. CHS, Justin Roberts. Justin was your typical high school hero. He was everything from the class president, to varsity football, to starting pitcher, to ASB activities director and his parents were even teachers at the school. He was the classic cool guy. In my marketing mind, I knew that he would be the key ingredient for campus success.

I approached him in the hallway next to some lockers, "Hey Justin!"

"Wassup brotha?" He said with a slap to the hand and a bump to the knuckles.

"Hey man, I just started a clothing company and I want to sponsor you. It's called Dickweed!"

He laughed, "That's rad, I'll sport 'em no problem. How can people buy them?"

I thought for a moment, and then recognized another opportunity, "From you," I said, figuring that people would buy more from him than they would me. "Sell them for fifteen bucks and I'll give you five for every shirt you sell."

"Sweet," he said in agreement.

The next day he sold fifteen shirts within a matter of hours. I was excited. This crazy shirt idea was taking off.

Brady attended North High on the other side of town. People liked the shirts there as well, but Brady wasn't into selling. He gave away just as many shirts as he sold.

Within two weeks, all the shirts were gone. I surveyed the students asking them what should be the next item in the Dickweed line up, and they all agreed that long sleeves were the next big thing.

A week later, we had a box of a hundred long sleeve shirts, and sure enough, they went just as quickly. By mid October, you couldn't walk around on campus without seeing a Dickweed shirt on somebody.

My school also had a work experience program, so I approached the teacher and asked, "If I'm the owner of a business, can I be in the program?"

He looked puzzled, "I don't know, we've never had that situation before. I don't see why not."

So, I signed up for the class and became the first student to own his own business, and thus I was able to give myself a grade, which of course, was always an +A. I'd even write sarcastic little notes next to the evaluation form; something along the lines of *John has been a wonderful worker, he deserves extra credit.*

In between classes, I'd exchange shirts for money with my sales reps, which had now extended to five people. I had everyone from jocks to skaters wearing and selling shirts.

As with anything that becomes popular, there is always opposition that arises. Teachers began sending students to the dean's office stating that the word Dickweed was inappropriate for clothing and was thus a distraction. Soon, students had to turn their shirts inside out. I couldn't help but laugh.

Not only did teachers begin complaining, but so did the parents. Apparently the dean's office began getting angry phone calls from parents saying that their kid had come home wearing a Dickweed shirt. But as the opposition from the establishment of parents and rigid teachers increased, so did the sales. Thus proving the marketing theory that people always want what they're not supposed to have.

As Dickweed continued to escalate, Brady called me up one day, "Hey man, I think I just want to sell you my part of the business."

"Why?" I asked.

"I don't know, I just want to ride dirt bikes, this business and selling stuff really isn't me, ya know?"

"Alright," I said, so I paid him three hundred bucks and took over as full owner of the business and sponsored him with shirts as he began doing freestyle motocross.

As winter approached, I extended the clothing line to hooded sweatshirts. Once again, they sold well, and sure enough, the resistance increased even more.

With the controversy on campus becoming more evident on a daily basis, the school editor approached me for an interview.

"Hey Mr. Dickweed," Jana Christensen said sarcastically.

I smirked, "Hey."

"Would you be willing to do an interview for our school paper?"

"Would I? Are you kidding, of course I would!" I exclaimed wanting further exposure.

"Great! Meet me in the library during third period." She told me.

I met her later that day and we conducted the interview. She asked me how it got started, what it meant, what I planned on doing with it and what I thought about the opposition from the faculty.

"I'm not out to hurt anybody. It's just a word on a shirt, it doesn't mean anything related to sex or drugs, although parents and teachers are trying to interpret it that way. What it really comes down to is freedom of speech, freedom of self-expression. The administration is trying to rob the students of expressing themselves, so I continue to fight back by selling more shirts," I grinned trying my best to sound like a reformist.

As we were half way through our interview, the dean walked in and Jana waved him over for a face-to-face confrontation.

Jana introduced us and he immediately put on his political façade answering all the questions with "the administration's best interest in mind."

"We are a public school and our best interest is for the students' unobstructed learning. We feel that *those* shirts are inappropriate for the classroom." He said, referring to Dickweed as *those* shirts.

I laughed and emphasized *Dickweed*, "So my *Dickweed* shirts are that much of a distraction, eh?"

"It just isn't appropriate to wear *those* shirts," he said officially on behalf of the administration's policy, "because it distracts the students from learning. I have no problem if people wear *those* shirts outside of school, but they aren't allowed on campus due to educational distraction."

Trying to sound like a leader of my imaginary revolution, I retorted, "Have you heard of freedom of speech? *Dickweed* shirts are a matter of self-expression, and if you prohibit students from expressing themselves, you're going to see an uprising!"

"This is a captive audience," he said with a matter-of-fact tone of voice. "Students aren't allowed to express themselves if it distracts other students from learning, bottom line." Then he walked away.

I tried saying something as he walked away, but he wouldn't have it. He had stated the administration's policy, without leaving any room for negotiation. Jana and I laughed as she scribbled down notes on a pad of paper.

"This is going to be a great interview," she said smiling brightly.

"Sweet," I said with a grin. "When is it going to come out in the paper?"

She put the pencil to her lip as she thought, "Probably after Christmas break, so the first week we get back from school."

"Nice," I beamed. After the interview, she took a few pictures of me, and then we went our separate ways.

Through Christmas break, I sold more shirts, long sleeves and sweatshirts. Everyone from relatives to neighbors bought shirts and my confidence continued to increase.

After Christmas break, the school paper came out. I ran over and grabbed one, fumbling through the pages looking for the article. To my surprise, Jana made it a full-page story. I smiled as I read the interview until I got to the last line, which read, *"During winter recess, the school administration has unanimously voted to ban the line of clothing. All students in violation will be sent home on first offense, and will be suspended thereafter."*

I was outraged! The Kern High School District had a meeting exclusively because of my clothing line. I was not informed and all the board members voted to ban my shirts from campus. The dean had made his political attack.

What a *Dick*...weed.

People came up to me after the article to show their support, "John, dude, you should like have a strike or something."

"Yeah, you're right, I should!" I shouted. It sounded like a good idea, but nobody wanted to join me when I tried to plan a student sit-out. I figured we could picket outside the school with signs that said, "WE WANT DICKWEED!" But everyone chickened out. Bummed and broken, I was being forced to give up the fight for Dickweed. So I looked for something else to do.

Justin Roberts came up to me with the bright idea of starting another clothing line, just a little less risqué, "Dude, I was thinkin' of a new name. Check it out, what do you think of Kirklen?"

I raised an eyebrow, "Kirklen?"

"Yeah, dude, Kirklen Clothing. Doesn't that sound cool?"

I figured that Justin was cool, so I thought that the name was cool, although I had no idea at the time that it was similar to a Costco brand name. I immediately went into production without marketing the idea to other students and when the shirts came out, I couldn't even give them away.

"That sucks," people told me point blank. "I wouldn't buy that."

Even more devastated because I couldn't sell or even give the shirts away, I began to slip back into my repressed depression. Thoughts of my mother's death started swimming around my head, and I began to retract.

However, people were still wearing their Dickweed shirts around school, although they were under constant threat of being sent home. I figured that if I could find a loophole around the administration's policy, then I could do Dickweed again.

One day in Spring I was walking down the hall and saw two security guards driving their golf cart towards me. They were the ones that were supposed to enforce the dean's decision to ban the clothing line, so they stopped me as they saw my Dickweed shirt.

"You're not supposed to wear that," they smirked half-heartedly.

"So you guys are anti-Dickweed, too, eh?"

They looked at each other, somewhat mellow because nobody was around, then answered, "We don't care. We'd wear one of those shirts, we think it's funny. The dean is just trying to play hardball. Frankly, we think it's cool what you're doing."

"Really?" I said somewhat surprised as my marketing mind began to kick in. "So you guys would wear a shirt, huh?"

They nodded, "Sure, we think it's funny."

"Well, tell you what, let's just say you turn a blind eye to the students wearing my shirts, and I'll give you shirts for free, how about that?"

They looked at each other and laughed, "Sure. We don't like the dean anyway."

"Sweet!" I said smiling and shaking their hands to seal the deal, then I went to my truck and got them their shirts. "So, you're not going to bust anyone right?"

They held up the shirts to their chest and grinned, "Nah, as far as we're concerned we haven't seen them."

Victory!

Now that I had the dean's "enforcement" on my side, I decided to fire back on the administration and release a new design for Spring break. This time, I'd really get their panties in a twist…literally!

Since Dickweed was named after a wiener dog, I took a clipart of a wiener dog and put it on the back of a shirt with the slogan, "WANNA PET MY WIENER?" To further poke my finger at the administration's rigid policy, I put a logo on the front of the shirt which read, "WARNING: DICKWEED: EXPLICIT CLOTHING."

Not only did I make shirts with the wiener dog logo; I also made matching boxer shorts to go along with it. To promote my new design I put the shirt on in the parking lot and put the boxers over my pants and walked around school. Everyone took notice and began laughing. Not only were they laughing, but they were also buying! I sold out within three days!

The administration was furious and they were threatening immediate suspension to anyone caught wearing the shirts. But mysteriously, students were never found wearing the shirts on campus. For some odd reason unknown to the administration, the security guards never seemed to see people wearing the shirts. Teachers, however, were sending students to the dean's office nearly everyday, yet, the dean never suspended them, thus proving that his bark was louder than his bite.

Dickweed had prevailed!

I figured that he was hoping that this Dickweed madness would end when I graduated in June. He didn't want a bigger mess than he already had, so he folded his cards. Dickweed survived!

In June, the dean got his wish. I stood in line with the graduating class of '99, and saw the dean standing near the stage. He nodded at me and I smirked and shrugged my shoulders. My economics teacher Mr. Wells and my history teacher Mr. Richmond, both Dickweed supporters, shouted and applauded, "Hey Dickweed! We wanna see you make a million by the time you're thirty!" I nodded my head, grabbed my diploma and headed into my promising future with a confident smile.

CHAPTER
FOURTEEN

(Freestyle rider and best friend, Brady Lambert)

"Moving on..."

The shadows of summer were longer than usual. I sat on my dirt bike and **stare**d at Brady's bright green punk rock hair and oversized pierced ears. His elbows rested on the handlebars as he looked at me with bold brown eyes and electric eyebrows.

"So you're moving down to your dad's, huh?"

"Yeah, I'm going to Cal State Fullerton in September, so I'm going to move down to my dad's in Corona Del Mar right before my birthday."

"Where's Corona Del Mar?"

"It's the Orange County area, a few miles south of Newport."

"Really? That'll be cool."

"Yeah, but I'm kind of nervous."

"Why?" Brady asked.

"I don't know," I hesitated. "I've grown up in Bakersfield since I was five. I've lived in the same house for the past twelve years. This is my home; I'm comfortable here. Corona Del Mar is a completely different world, not to mention that I've never lived with my dad before. It's just a big change, ya know?"

"Yeah, that's true," Brady related, "but it will be good for you to get out of Bakersfield. Why would you want to stay here when you can be chillin' at the beach, bro?"

I thought for a moment then laughed, "Yeah, you're right. I guess it's just going to be different. It just sucks that I'm not going to be here in Bakersfield with all my friends for my eighteenth birthday that kind of bums me out."

Brady's voice dropped, "Dude, that sucks." Then he thought for a moment and grinned, "I guess we'll just have to throw you a fatty party before you leave."

"That'd be sweet," I smiled.

"When are you leaving?" he asked.

"August 11th, the day before my birthday."

"Alright, we'll party it up on the tenth, how does that sound?"

"Sweet," I said.

"It's crazy man," he said looking sad, "Everybody's growing up and moving on."

I nodded numbly. "We're all growing up…it's crazy man, we're going to be 18 soon, you know what that means?"

"What? We can buy cigarettes and porn?" He smarted.

"Well, that too, I guess, but we're going to be adults, responsibility and all that stuff." I said staring into the setting sun.

He cringed and chuckled, "Uh, that's scary bro. I don't like that word. I'm like Peter Pan, I never wanna grow up!"

I smirked and nodded.

"Wanna ride some more before we have to grow up and move on?" He asked sliding his helmet back on.

"Sure, let's hit it," I said kick starting my dirt bike.

He took off in front of me and launched over a hundred foot double, whipping his bike sideways and looked back at me in mid-air. I revved my bike up the face of the jump and did the same, looking back into the blue sky of the past…and flying, flying, flying into the future of adulthood, responsibility, and everything else that was so damn scary, so distant and so unknown.

On August 10th, I gathered up my closest buddies Daniel, Brady, JD, Torrance and Cole. Daniel drove my new truck that my dad had bought me for graduation, as Brady told us his plan for the night's activities.

"Check it out fellas," he said pulling out a zip lock bag filled halfway with dried mushrooms, "we're going to shroom our heads off!" He said following through with a mischievous laugh.

I looked at the other guys in the truck nervously; they all smiled and laughed.

.

Daniel looked at me looking at him, "Dude, don't look at me!" he said defensively, "I'm the designated driver."

I had never done drugs before, so I had no idea what to expect. The nervous look on my face must have been obvious. "Don't worry bro," Brady said calmly, "you'll have fun. You'll just be in a different world for about six hours; you'll see life like you've never seen it before. Trust me, it'll be fun."

"Alright," I said, "but where are we going to do them?"

"I dunno," Brady shrugged his shoulders while giving the mushrooms to everyone except Daniel.

"We can go to Breckenridge road," Daniel suggested, "it's up in the mountains, you guys can trip out up there."

"Sounds good," Brady laughed.

With a nervous smile, I shrugged my shoulders.

I **stare**d at the palm of my hand as Brady put a pile of dried stems and brown mushroom caps into it.

"Isn't that a lot?" I asked.

"Yeah," he grinned, "but it's your party, consider it your birthday present."

The guys in the back seat of my truck all began munching the crunchy mushrooms. Their faces eager for the experience yet bitter from the taste. I looked at Brady as he poured the rest of the bag into his hand, "Bottoms up," he said.

Putting the handful of mushrooms into my mouth, I began chewing with the same look of bitterness on my face. "They taste like rotten sunflower seeds," I said with full cheeks. Brady and the rest of the guys laughed.

The drive up the twisty mountain took nearly thirty minutes. The lights of the city disappeared as we drove deeper into the darkness of the woods. Everyone in the truck was quiet, each of us were anticipating what was about to happen. The lit dashboard of my truck began to radiate with a green glow unlike anything I had seen before. I began to giggle.

Brady laughed, "You feelin' it Butler?"

"Where are we going, going, going?" I asked as I escaped my body through an echo.

Daniel looked at me, his head four times larger than before, "We're almost there, there, there, there," his voiced reverberated through a vortex of time.

A few more twists and turns then he pulled over. I got out of my truck as if I was getting out of a spaceship, "We're on Mars!" I exclaimed with a wavy voice.

The three guys in the back seat, JD, Cole and Torrance got out and ran down the road shouting, "We're on Mars! We're on Mars!"

My wide eyes looked at Brady through the darkness; his body wavered and stretched uncontrollably. I looked up at the night sky and saw the stars swirl around like the galaxy was spinning in a blender. The blackness of the night began to change into purple, then green, before fizzling into fascinating colors unknown to the human eye. The silent shadows shifted in the background; "We're surrounded by wolves!" Someone screamed.

Taking over-exaggerated steps as if I was a detective, I began exploring my new environment. Brady walked in front of me twirling like a tornado; his flying arms left tracers of flesh. Daniel walked closely behind us, making sure we didn't jump off a cliff.

JD, Torrance and Cole came running toward us, the three of them trapped in a psychedelic delusion, "We have to go back," they said panicked, "there's wolves out here!"

Brady and I started running back towards the truck with them, although we were laughing hysterically as we feared for our lives.

"HEI, I Y'AI, AH, YA'IY!" Brady howled like a hyena.

Daniel drove our spaceship back to Bakersfield. The ride down the mountain felt like we were plummeting in a rocket down to earth. We screamed with our arms raised as if riding a roller coaster.

Once in town, the lights and billboards near the side of the road danced around like cartoons. My physical body was nonexistent; the psychedelic had overloaded my sensations.

"Hey, do you guys mind if I stop by the Vu?" Daniel asked, "I want to see if a chick I know is dancing there tonight."

We didn't care where we went; we were somewhere else, in a world far, far away. Daniel drove us over to the female dance club and left us in the truck, "Don't get out guys, I'll be right back."

I sat in the passenger seat and started rolling down the window while laughing loudly like a witch. Then I **stare**d at Brady's face, which was liquid like water and watched his smile swim around his head, and then I asked, "Why is the window up?" Then I'd roll the window up, and ask, "Why is the window down?" He exploded into laughter, which I saw erupt like streaks of light. The three guys in the back seat of the truck sat silent with swimming smiles of their own. I repeatedly rolled the window up, then down again, until the bouncers in front of the club began to take notice.

"Butler, calm down, those guys are staring at us," Brady cautioned in mid-chuckle.

I glared towards the bouncers' direction and pointed at them, "You guys are aliens!" I shouted out the window, then I was washed away with laughter once again.

Daniel noticed that we were making a huge commotion outside, so he whisked us away to his place.

When we walked into his house, the walls began to breathe in and out as the ceilings stretched sideways, making the house feel like a mansion one second, then like a shack the next. Our senses were completely out of whack.

By now, the psychedelic mushrooms had completely taken over our bodies and minds. I chased Daniel's dog around the house trying to talk to it. Brady, JD, Cole and Torrance sat on the couch then shouted; "We're sinking! We're sinking!"

I then fell to the floor and watched the ceiling collapse into different colors becoming mesmerized by the dancing walls inside the house. After a few hours of this madness, the mushrooms finally wore off. The five of us became quiet from mental exhaustion, and Daniel drove us home.

As Daniel dropped off the other guys, I became lost inside my head. Thoughts made conversations with my memories, as my mind became a playground for psychological exploration. I thought about my life and my mother's death. Images of her face floated through my mind, yet I couldn't comprehend that it was her. I realized that I still had not accepted that she was truly gone.

My thoughts began to taunt me as I started to dwell on the denial of her death. Losing my mind that night made me feel even more lost. Who was I? Where was I going? What was I doing? All of these questions began to bubble up from my brain. Yet, I didn't have any answers, so I slipped away on a sea of suppressed sadness…a terrible trance to become trapped in the day before leaving for college.

CHAPTER
FIFTEEN

"*Clouds of comfort...*"

The gold clock on her oak desk is clicking off the cost of my thoughts. Her Ph.D. in Psychology hangs on the wall as a symbol of social and educational achievement.

Outside her window, beyond her gray hair, is a solitary orange leaf lingering on a naked tree limb. A cold September breeze blows a cotton cloud across a changing sky. She is looking at me through her glasses. I am staring *through* her at the cloud.

"So, you haven't cried since your mother died?" She asks breaking the silence.

I **stare** at her blankly, "No."

She thinks and analyzes, "Why not?"

I **stare** through her, and then I shrug my shoulders, "I don't know, I just haven't."

She scribbles something down on her note pad, perhaps something along the lines that I am crazy and that I am emotionally insane and perhaps that I will need a lifetime of therapy, and she, being my therapist, will be utterly rich. Yes, she will capitalize on my pain. She will pick and prod my mind, my heart and my soul until I am nothing more than a weekly paycheck.

"And when you saw your mother lying there in the casket, how did that make you feel?"

'*Feel*?' I think absurdly to myself. How was I supposed to *feel* looking at my dead mother? Was there an appropriate feeling to be *felt*?

Sad?

Abandoned?

Despondent?

My **stare** now burns through her and her Ph.D. hanging on the wall. I sit on her leather couch and watch her watch me. I can dance within the silence of my soul.

She cannot see me. I am invisible.

She is talking to thin air. She is writing notes on nothing because I am nothing. Her office is empty because I am empty.

She looks at me. She is waiting for an answer.

'*Feel..?...Feel?...hmm, this is a tricky one,*' I am thinking to myself. I see my dead mother lying in a casket and I am supposed to *feel* something? I feel nothing because I am nothing. I feel not because I am not.

"I didn't feel anything," I blurt out, unsure if that is a suitable answer.

She looks at me. She doesn't just look at me, but she gives me *the look*. The look is judging, analyzing, scrutinizing, dissecting. The look is memorizing the miserable mess which I call my life, so that she can write a book about it someday, and from that book she will make millions of dollars, and she will buy a yacht which she will tie next to her dock on her own private island as she sips cocktails from a coconut with a little pink umbrella sticking out of it and she will tell my life story as a joke to rich people named Buffy and Babsy.

She then looks at me, after scribbling more notes, with a different look. The look as if my head is a dollar sign. *'Yes, yes, this is good,'* she must be thinking to herself, *'this poor, poor child who lost his mother to cervical cancer. He is a psychological mess, and I will analyze him and I will capitalize on him, forever and ever, and I can finally buy that yacht....'* Certainly, this is what she must be thinking of me when she gives me *that look.*

I know this because I am eighteen and I know everything.

She is an old psychologist and she knows nothing.

She puts her finger to the side of her face and tilts her head with concern, "Why do you think you didn't feel anything?"

'You're the freaking psychologist!' the voice inside my head screams, *'Aren't you supposed to be answering these questions? Why the hell is my Dad paying you?'*

I sit and **stare**. The timer on her desk is clicking away our sixty minute session, *click, click, click.* With each click, I imagine that I am being carried away on a cloud. *Click, click, click,* there goes John, *click, click, click,* floating away from this office on a cloud. Wave goodbye to the psychologist, John, float away, you don't need her. *Click, click, click...*

"I guess, umm," I am thinking of an answer because she wants an answer. "I guess I was just numb. I didn't really think that she was going to die."

"But you knew that she was sick, right?"

She is poking. She is prodding. She is trying to pop my fickle emotional façade.

"Well, yeah. She was sick for a year and half," I tried to explain myself. "I mean, I knew that she was going to die, but I guess I just didn't believe that she really would."

She is scribbling notes; I am floating away...*click, click, click.*

"So it was hard for you to actually accept your mother's death?"

Bells and whistles go off inside my brain. The game show host inside my head sarcastically says, *'Bingo! Let's give this lady a prize! She's a freaking genius! Tell her what she's won John!'*

"Of course it was hard." I say bluntly like she's an idiot.

"Have you accepted it yet?"

Damn her and her damned questions. *Click, click, click...*my cloud is drifting further and further away.

"I guess so," I say shrugging my shoulders.

She gives me *the look.*

"Do you think that is why you are having a hard time adjusting to living with your dad in Corona Del Mar and trying to go to college? Does it seem too hard to adjust because you haven't put closure on your mother's death?"

My guts are churning. I picture my bloody beating heart thumping against my chest. I feel water building behind my eyeballs, but I breathe deeply and **stare** through the wall. My x-ray vision allows me to penetrate through buildings. My **stare** singes all those who stand in my way. I can see through trees, buildings, anything and everything, until I see my cloud. It is waiting. I climb aboard my cozy cloud of comfort and I float away...click, click, click.

"Well, living down here is completely different," I tell her as I climb aboard my cloud. "I tried going to school for the first few weeks, but the school is too big. I feel lost. In Bakersfield, everyone knew who I was. Down here in southern California, everyone is too busy and chaotic. I feel lost."

She thinks, then she scribbles some more. I want to take her scribbling pad and slap her with it.

"So, would you say that you have a lost sense of self-identity since your mother passed away?"

Where is my cloud? I am falling from the sky. My cloud has left me. I am dropping like a dime from heaven. Her sophisticated psychological mumbo jumbo is bringing me down.

"I guess so. She was everything to me. My mother was the queen of my world. I loved her very much, that is why I feel bad that I haven't cried. Is that wrong?"

I turn the question to her because I am clever. Yes, I am clever and I am smarter than she is. I will make her earn the hundred dollars she is milking from my dad for this one-hour session, yes! I will make her answer *my* questions.

She thinks as she looks at the scribbling on her pad.

Oh, she is good, too good.

She is milking the clock for every second, refusing to give me any answers so I will come back again and again and again and again-

"No," she answers as I am ranting and raving inside my head. "There is nothing wrong, in fact, it is often quite normal for people to experience some form of denial when someone close to them has died. But I think that it is important that you recognize that you are struggling with denial, so that you can continue on with the grieving process or else it will emotionally cripple you from other things in life such as going to school and moving away."

Oh, she is good. She is too good.

But my **stare** is better. My **stare** can burn through her brain and she doesn't even know it.

"So what am I supposed to do about it, cry?" I slam the ball back into her court so that she must answer me again.

But she is quick, too quick, "Yes, crying would be good. There is nothing wrong with crying and recognizing that someone very close and very special to you, your mother, has passed away. Blocking your feelings and denying that she is gone doesn't damage anyone but yourself."

Her face is on fire. My **stare** has set her aflame. She doesn't feel it, but I know that she is burning and soon she will run out of the office screaming that her face is on fire, and I, the almighty fire-starting-**stare**-giver will be victorious.

"I have tried to cry," I say. "But it won't come out, so how am I supposed to get over her death?" Oh, I am good, too good. Let's see her answer this one.

"Well," she says before taking a long pause. She consults her notes, which are now making me increasingly paranoid. "Maybe taking a photo album to her graveside and sharing out loud some memories that you have of her will bring about some emotions."

I shrug my shoulders at her mediocre suggestion.

"I've gone to her graveside," I say slamming her suggestion down to the office floor.

"How did you *feel*?"

There's that damn *feel* word again. Why must she keep bringing that up? Doesn't she know that I am a man and that I have been trained and sculpted by society not to feel? Yes, I am a hunter brought up by other hunting males. I have been bred to be an unemotional warrior so that I do not fold under the pressures of emotional battles. I want to stand up on her desk and tear my shirt open and beat my chest like Tarzan.

I am brave.

I am a warrior.

I do not cry because I do not feel.

I am invincible!

"I felt, uhh," I say searching for the right words to her wronged question. "I felt, uhh, fine."

'Fine? Where did that one come from?' I think condemning myself for giving her more leverage.

"You felt *fine*?" She asks giving me the look.

"I mean, not fine, but you know…I mean…I felt okay."

She raises her eyebrows and gives me the look again, "You felt *okay*?"

"Well, not okay, but, uh, I don't know, I didn't feel anything, isn't that okay?"

The look has engulfed my entire existence within her office. She is looking at me. I am staring at her. The face off seems to last forever.

Her look is analyzing, condemning, judging.

My **stare** is attacking, conquering, justifying.

She writes something on her scribbling pad. Now I am panicking that she hasn't been writing anything at all.

No.

I now fear that she has been drawing goofy stick figured pictures of me indicating that I am a wacko. I want to stand up and steal the pad out of her hands and surely I will see a sketch of me with little weird symbols over my body signifying that, I, John Butler, am indeed, a freak.

"You are obviously struggling to come to terms with her death," she says. "I think it might be best if you were to take some time off from your first semester at Fullerton. Take some time for yourself; allow yourself to grieve her death. Perhaps spend sometime in Bakersfield so you can put closure on the things that need to be taken care of. Otherwise, you are going to find yourself in a continued cycle of self-defeat because you will constantly feel as though your life is incomplete."

Oh, she is good, too good.

"So you're telling me to quit school?" I say somewhat keen to the idea.

"No, not quit school. Just take this semester off, take sometime to grieve, and then reenroll for next semester." She says as her diagnosis.

"Hmm, that sounds good." I say feeling justified now that I have an excuse not to go to school.

The clock is clicking...click, click, click. She looks at me looking at the clock.

Out of curiosity she asks, "What are you thinking about when you look at the clock?"

CRAP! I have been caught. She must know that I am floating away on a cloud. How could she tell? Did my distant eyes give my destination away?

"What do you mean?" I say trying to disguise my self-vacancy. "I was just seeing how much time we have left." Oh, I am clever.

"I have been watching you look at the clock, and when you do, your face changes, as if you aren't here anymore." Oh, she is better, she is way better.

I smile awkwardly, "I...uh, just, um, don't know. I was just looking at the clock, that's all." I say sticking to my first defense, because I am the best, yes, I am indeed the best in the entire world.

"Well, is there anything else you would like to discuss before we end this session?" She says wrapping up my exploded emotional damage in a neat little package because she is a professional.

I shrug my shoulders and shake my head side-to-side.

She stops the timer on her desk, yet the clicking inside my head continues. I climb on to my cloud and float out of her office and into my world where her questions will never get me again…I am the cloud…I have floated away…I am floating above the city, across the ocean, beyond the stars and into the sun…yes, I am the best…I am the best damn cloud to ever float away.

CHAPTER SIXTEEN

(Father and Son)

"Leaving the kingdom…"

I am flying through the October sky; the Pacific Ocean is a blue painting on the untouchable horizon. Mercedes and BMWs transport beautiful tan people to marvelous marble buildings such as banks, malls, and corporate skyscrapers. People carry small dogs under their arms; their poodles are better dressed than I am. I take a deep breath and smell the ocean air. It smells like money.

Corona Del Mar, the planet of which I am not a part of, is a hub of rich people. These are not just rich people, but people so rich that they can buy you and will make you their gardener, just so they can laugh at you to their friends as they sip on tea in the afternoon. However they just don't laugh like us normal middle class people, no; they laugh softly with an open mouth so they can show off how pearly white their teeth are. And, as they do, they bring their hands to their chest, palms facing themselves, so that you can see all of their jewelry. Yes, they do this; they do this to me, the kid from Bakersfield who lost his mother, so that I will know that one of their rings is worth more money than I will ever make in my entire life. Yes, this is Corona Del Mar, the planet of the rich people.

I am not rich. I am from Bakersfield.

I am an alien in this greedy world. This is their planet…not mine.

Driving down Pacific Coast Highway, I am reciting things inside my head; things that I will tell my dad, things like: *'So dad, you know, I've been thinking that I should move back to Bakersfield, umm, yeah, Bakersfield, because, umm, because the psychologist suggested that I, uh, grieve. Yes, she said that I should move to Bakersfield and grieve, yes, grieve, crying all that kind of stuff. You understand, right dad? Grieving? I know, I know, school is important, but isn't my emotional well being more important?'*

I replay the script in my mind over and over again.

The sun is shining and it is seventy-five degrees.

Why? Because it is southern California and it is *always* seventy-five degrees that's why. I am driving my brand new Dodge truck to my dad's oceanfront office in San Juan Capistrano. He is an Internet guru. He is an automotive genius. He is a hero, my hero. Yes, he is my dad. His cape flaps in the wind as he puts both of his fists on his hips while he walks on water.

Walking into his office, I see his assistant Lorene. I like Lorene; she makes me smile because she says that I am handsome. Yes, I am handsome. She said so, therefore, I must be.

"You're so handsome," she says as I walk up to her desk. See I told you she tells me that I am handsome, didn't you believe me?

"Is my dad available," I say flashing my God-given dimples proving that her statement is indeed correct.

She smiles, "Hold on sweetie, let me check." She picks up the phone and tells my dad that I am there to see him. I look around the office; the white walls serve as backgrounds for fancy framed articles that my father has inspired. It is my dad's empire. Yes, my dad is a king. He has ladies that call him on the intercom and say that I am here to see him. My dad is the king. I am a prince. Together, we are royalty.

"Go ahead," Lorene says with a wink and smile. I flash her my dimples once more. She giggles.

I walk to the back where my dad's office is. His name is written next to the door in gold, *'John J. Butler III, Director of Marketing and Sales.'*

I knock on the door with my knuckle as I push the door open.

He is sitting on a leather throne talking on the phone to a peasant. He has a crown of silver hair. His face is aged with wisdom. He is my twin. I **stare** at him and I see my future. He **stare**s at me and he sees his past. We are clones; royal clones that will one day rule the world.

When I walk into the room he smiles and gestures silently with his hand that it will just be a second.

I nod.

To the side of his desk I see a sliding glass door, which overlooks the Pacific Ocean. I **stare** *through* the blue horizon. White waves crash against a blonde beach. I see a cotton cloud in the sky and I dream of floating away-

"Hey-hey Johnny boy. What's happening?" My dad says proudly. My dad is proud of me because I am going to Cal State Fullerton. I am a jewel in his crown.

"Hey pops," I say with a bright yet nervous smile.

He gestures to a chair in front of his desk, "Have a seat."

I sit down and swipe my sweaty palms on my knees, "Dad, um, I was thinking."

He smirks, "Thinking is a good thing."

I smile hesitantly, "Right, it is a good thing. I was thinking that I, uh, want to move up to Bakersfield."

His face freezes with a smile.

I continue, "Um, yeah, I don't think living down here is *my thing*, ya know?"

He is still smiling. Behind his smile, I see his mind working overtime. He is scrambling to think of an appropriate response.

"Well," he says slowly, "what about school?"

"Yeah, school. Um, I don't know if Fullerton is really for me. The psychologist said that maybe taking some time off from school and taking some time to grieve my mom's death might help with the lack of motivation that I have been struggling with since moving down here."

He nods his head as he holds his chin with his forefinger. He is thinking because he is a brilliant thinker.

"I see."

"I mean, I like living with you, but Bakersfield is where my heart is. I mean, I don't want to quit school forever, but maybe just take off this semester so I can get my head straight, then I'll reenroll next semester…in Bakersfield."

"I see," he says with quiet wisdom.

My palms are sweaty. My stomach is empty. I want to jump out the window and land on my cloud. He is thinking. He is thinking while he is smiling. Oh, he is good. He is too good.

"Well," he says carefully, "if that is what you want to do then I support you."

"You do?" I say somewhat surprised, "I mean, you're not disappointed that I'm not going to go to Fullerton?"

"No. Fullerton is just a school. I want you to do what you think is best." He says with supportive wisdom. "This is your life. The decisions you make now are going to have effects either way. But it is up to you to decide which paths you will take in life."

Yes, my dad is the wisest king in all the kingdoms.

He is my dad. My dad is a king, yes, he is indeed a wise king.

We stand up and he hugs me. I look into his eyes, and although he is a wise king, I can't help but see a shadow of disappointment in the edges of his smile.

I open the sliding glass door and climb onto the balcony railing as I spread my arms like wings. Then I look back and say, "Bye dad!"

"Bye!" He says with a sad shadow of a smile.

Then I launch myself off the balcony and into the sky and fly like a bird above all the clouds of the kingdom.

CHAPTER
SEVENTEEN

(John and step mom Maryknoll)

"Stoned stoopid…"

I have called my step dad Dave in Bakersfield and I have made arrangements to move back home. He is not happy about my decision, but, as long as I promise to reenroll at Cal State Bakersfield in January, he will let me move back home.

I am thrilled. I will come back home to Bakersfield and everyone will throw me a parade. People will line the streets as my truck pulls into town and they will throw confetti and young girls will scream like I am Elvis. All of the city officials will come and meet me because I was brave enough to leave town for three months in an attempt to go to college somewhere else. The mayor will give me a key to the city and I will raise it above my head in triumph. My picture will be on the cover of *The Californian* and the title will read: DICKWEED, OUR HOMETOWN HERO RETURNS!

I pull up to my house and there is no parade. Perhaps people forgot, oh well. I don't care because I am happy to be home.

Before I left Corona Del Mar, I met with a lady who was once my stepmother, Maryknoll, and she gave me $2,000 dollars which she had set aside in an investment portfolio when I graduated. While I was down in Corona Del Mar, I stayed up late at night and made Dickweed designs and business plans, which I presented to Maryknoll stating that I could use the $2,000 for my business. She graciously complied.

Now that I was back in Bakersfield in early November, I set my sights into more Dickweed production. I contacted a screen printer and ordered t-shirts, long sleeves and sweatshirts for the upcoming holiday season. He told me it would be done in early December, so I had a little less than a month in which I had to keep myself occupied.

The good thing was that the run of shirts would only cost me about half of my two-grand. The bad thing was, I had a thousand dollars to keep myself entertained with. While I was in Corona Del Mar, I worked in a video store. The manager of the store was a big pothead, and after work he and I would go get stoned. And seeing that I had a thousand bucks left over, as well as some time to kill, I decided that the most responsible and logical thing I could do, and should do, was to buy pot. Yes, I am eighteen, and I know what is responsible and logical, and that is buying pot. Lots of pot.

I drove around Bakersfield in my new truck and

smoked like I was Cheech and Chong, except, I was by myself, therefore I could be both Cheech and Chong at the same time. Needless to say, I was really high.

My step dad Dave would have skinned me like a snake had he known I returned home with this new habit, so I did what any typical stoned teenager would do; I would stay out really, really late and come home after he was already in bed. Remember that I am eighteen and I am responsible and logical, so this is what I did. Makes sense, right?

As I smoked pot, lots of pot, I found a hazy cloud that would let me hide my problems. *'I am hurting about my mother,'* I'd say to the bong. Then I would smoke. *'I'm really depressed about her death,'* I'd say to the joint. Then I would smoke. Rather than face my problems head on, I'd dive into the bottom of a bong. Rather than cry and grieve in a healthy rational manner, I would smoke myself numb so I wouldn't feel pain. I do not like confrontation. I do not like pain. Confrontation is painful. Denial was easier. Smoking pot made denial seem that much easier. Besides, it smelled good.

The days of November danced away in a smoky daze. My life was becoming shallow and meaningless. The painful days of denial are lit with the lack of confrontation.

I didn't want to be alive anymore; I wanted to die. I was depressed, and no matter how much I smoked or how high I got, my problems were still there when I slipped back into the sobriety of a new day.

CHAPTER
EIGHTEEN

(Being interviewed by Channel 17 news at the Dickweed charity event, 1999)
"Feeding the hungry..."

It is December. I know that it is December because I can see my breath when I breathe, that, and because my shirts are done. I am excited.

In hopes of making the shirt sales successful, I plan on carrying out a charity event in front of one of my retailer's stores.

"Hey Ray," I say on the other side of a clothing rack in his store. He is Ray Crumb, a professional dirt bike rider that started his own clothing shop.

"What up, Butler? I thought you fell off the face of the earth, where've you been?" He asks with a silly smirk.

"Long story," I say trying to keep things to the point. "Hey, I got some new shirts out and I was thinking of doing a promotional event outside your store for charity."

"Sweet, like what?"

"Well," at this point I go into my promotional pitch fully demonstrated with my dramatic hands, "I was thinking of making peanut butter and jelly sandwiches for twenty-four hours while I sit on top of your roof. But not only will I make sandwiches, but we will collect clothes and money for the homeless."

He raises his eyebrows as I look at him with exuberant ambition.

"But this is the best part," I say with a sly smirk, "I'm going to make a Dickweed banner and it will say, *'Dickweed 24-hour stand off: Clothe the naked, feed the hungry and house the homeless!'* Then I'll have all the news stations come out and film it, it will be great!"

Again, he raises his eyebrows and gives me a silly grin, "Sweet," he says.

"So what do you think? Are you down?"

"Uh," he is thinking. "I guess so. I don't think you can sit on the roof, but other than that, I don't see why we couldn't. Sure, let's do it."

"That's all right," I say. "I can just stand on the sidewalk."

"When do you want to do it?" He asks.

"How about in two weeks?"

"Sounds good to me."

"Great!" I exclaim. The plan was now in motion.

I sent out press releases to all the news stations in town, including the newspaper and any other media related fax numbers that I could find as I prepared for the big day.

In my mind, I saw thousands of people thronging themselves to the store. Helicopters would buzz around and spotlights would be set in place. People, the generous and ever-giving people of Bakersfield, would fill the parking lot bringing all of their used clothes in truckloads. They would all be willing to give me hundreds, if not thousands of dollars in support, and they would all walk up to me with tears in their eyes, 'John, you are such a good person for doing this!' I would then nod my head with humbleness and say, 'I know, I know.' Sure enough, all of my shirts would be sold. Sounds reasonable, right?

As the day approached, I saw a handful of people. They were all my friends, the ones I had called just an hour before. A few of them brought clothes, but the others were there strictly because of the obligatory friendship law: "Whatever John does, we must support him, or else…"

"Are you really going to make peanut butter and jelly sandwiches for twenty-four hours," my friend Taylor asked.

Still confident that the crowds were going to file in any minute I said, "Of course."

He looked at my table set up on the sidewalk, then he asked, "Did you even bring peanut butter and jelly?"

I **stare**d at him. Then I **stare**d at the Channel 17 news van pulling up to the parking lot. "Um, no," I said starting to panic.

"Are you John Butler?" The cameraman asked.

"Yes, yes I am," I said shaking his hand. My exterior was calm and cool. My interior was flipping out screaming and squealing because I was unprepared and the cameraman was early.

"Well, we got your info about doing an event," he said looking around at me and my five buddies standing next to a fold out table with nothing on it except some Dickweed shirts. "Something about sandwiches…"

"Yes, yes," I say with a smooth smile trying to be professional. "The thing is, we have a person bringing the bread and materials any minute, so if you can give me just a few minutes we can set up."

"Alright, but I'm on a tight time schedule," he said walking back to his van to get his camera equipment.

"Jessica, I need you to run to the store across the street and get me some peanut butter and jelly material, bread, everything! Quick!"

She grabbed some money and ran to the store. She returned ten minutes later with the store brand material, "Sorry, there was a line," she said.

"Just give me the stuff," I said still panicked not wanting the cameraman to desert our poorly organized promotion.

The cameraman set up his equipment and said, "Alright. I want to get some footage of you making the sandwiches, then we'll do a little interview."

"Great!" I said fumbling with the bag of bread. I laid out a few pieces then popped open the jar of jelly and peanut butter.

"Alright, I'm ready when you are," the cameraman said as he focused squarely on the sandwiches.

I took a knife and spread some peanut butter on the bread. The only problem was, the peanut butter was so oily that it just oozed out of the jar like brown toxic waste. I am panicking, *'Oh, this is bad, this is so bad.'* My friends begin to snicker. The cameraman is focused.

I take the jelly, and it too oozes out in the most disgusting manner. My mind is now showing me flashes of the news cast, *'Young entrepreneur poisons homeless people with radioactive sandwiches...next at five.'*

I am humiliated. I am not only humiliated, but I am a monster. Yes, I am making sandwiches for hungry people, but I am feeding them poisonous goo.

The cameraman says abruptly, "Okay, that should be enough. Now we'll just do a *quick* interview then we will be done." He says the word *quick* really quickly.

He attaches a microphone to my shirt and I am then staring into a black lens mumbling something about the event, the shirts, and something about sandwiches; honestly, I don't even remember. Quite frankly, I don't want to remember. It was a failure, because I was a failure. I am doomed.

The cameraman finishes up and tells me that it will be on the five o'clock news. I tell him thanks, then as he leaves, I turn around and see my friends all inside the store dying with laughter.

Someone blurts out, "Those sandwiches are the worst thing I have ever seen!"

"Yeah, yeah. I know. Why did you buy the store brand stuff!" I turn to Jessica to shift the blame and self-guilt.

"That's all I could afford, don't blame me, it's your event. You should have brought your own stuff."

I couldn't argue.

Later that night, as I was on my two-hundredth sandwich, my friend comes by and says he saw the news spot. He told me that they showed it for about fifteen seconds, then they went to a segment about a kitten stuck in a tree, that and the fact that they said the event was happening at the wrong location across town.

I am devastated. I have failed.

Halfway through the night, I give up in total defeat. My friends sneak me away in their truck, and I leave the place of my failure in order that I can hide my defeat in a cloud of smoke.

The next morning I show up again, and finish out the event. In all I made about three hundred totally disgusting sandwiches that no human should've ever been forced to eat.

I collected a garbage bag full of clothes and sold a total of about ten shirts, all to my obligated friends of course.

I drove to the homeless shelter and dropped off the sandwiches, clothes and about ten bucks that someone's mom donated.

"Here you go," I said with a halfhearted smile.

The guy looked in the box full of sickly sandwiches, then he glared at me and said, "Gee, thanks."

At least I tried…at least *I tried.*

CHAPTER
NINETEEN

(John and Brady, 1999)

"Melting with Elmo..."

The week after my promotional flop, I got a phone call from Brady.

"Hey Butler, what are you doing Friday night?"

"I'm going to the movies with a chick, but I should be home about ten, why?"

"Well, I'm going to come over, cool?"

"That's fine," I said.

After my date, I drove to my house and saw that Brady was already there with two of his buddies. My step dad was out of town, and the three of them had plans to have some fun.

I greeted them at the door with a slap to the hand, "What's up fellas?"

They grinned.

"Hey Butler, I've got some chicks coming over, hope you don't mind."

I could tell by Brady's voice that he was up to something, "Why? What do you have planned?"

He grinned a little wider then said, "You'll see."

The four of us walked into the house and sat on the couch. Brady walked over to the kitchen counter and started separating something.

"What are you doing?" I asked.

"Oh, some of this, some of that," he laughed.

I walked over to where he was and saw some pills and strips of paper. He grinned the devilish grin that I knew all too well.

"No really, what is that?"

"Little bit of ecstasy and LSD," he said with a sinful smile.

Instantly I see a flash of the future: Dave comes home early from his trip and he sees all of us on drugs in his house. I see flames of fire fly from his eyes and he grows ten feet tall. Dave then grabs Brady and my friends and he rips their heads off with his teeth. I see myself backing into a corner saying 'no, no Dave, I'm sorry, please don't,' then he picks me up by my ears before body slamming my spine upon his knee, breaking every bone in my body. The wrath of my step dad will surely be felt.

"Dude, I don't think this is a good idea," I say to Brady as I snap back out of my sure-to-happen revelation.

He picks up a strip of paper from the countertop and says, "Here, put this on your tongue. Don't worry, Butler, it'll be fine."

"What will it do?" I ask grabbing the tiny strip from his pinched fingers.

He gives me the used-car salesman smile and says, "It's like the shrooms, just a little stronger."

I am holding the strip of paper; analyzing, contemplating, justifying.

Brady sees that I am still struggling with the decision, "It will help you think about things," he says. "It's a psychedelic. Your mind will think about things that you've never thought about."

My arm has been twisted, although not very hard, and I agree with his justification. *'Yeah, it will help me think about things, yeah, that's it. I'll think about things.'*

I put the piece of paper under my tongue. Brady and the two other guys take the pills of ecstasy and the other tabs of LSD.

We sit on the couch and watch TV as we wait for the girls to come over. I am trying to sit still. My knee is bouncing up and down like a jackhammer while I tap my fingers on my thigh.

What is going to happen?

When does this stuff work?

What is this stuff? What am I doing?

What if Dave comes home and kills us?

Surely he will kill us, yes, he will strangle me until I am blue in the face, my friends' bodies will be decapitated lying next to me, and it will all be my fault.

What the hell am I doing?

As we watch TV, I notice something on the wall. At first I think it is a shadow, but then I realize that it is dripping. My walls are melting. I blink profusely, unsure if I am really seeing what I think I saw.

Yes, there it goes again. The stucco pattern on the wall is liquid and it is slowly moving downward like a waterfall. I giggle and grin.

Brady hears my giggle and looks at me and laughs, "What up Butler? Feeling good?"

I can't stop smiling. My eyebrows are raised in amazement. I look at the blue swirling carpet. It is swimming around. My couch is now a boat and we are floating down a river into the TV. The wall is a white waterfall.

Brady and the other guys are all looking at different things in the room with their own form of fascination. We all giggle at different times and at different things.

"I think I'm melting," Brady says rubbing his face.

I look at him, and he is indeed melting. I worry that his melted flesh will stain the carpet, but then I realize that the carpet is constantly swirling, so I figure that his flesh won't stick. Good thing, too, because melted flesh on the carpet would be hard to explain to my step dad.

As I **stare** into the television I realize that I am looking through a portal into another universe. The people on TV are from another world and they are not acting, but they are living their lives in another dimension. I become fascinated with their fourth dimensional reality.

Suddenly we hear three pounding thuds: Thud, thud, thud. It echoes through the house. Instantly I know that it is my step dad who has come to demolish us in our drugged delusions. I jumped up and looked for somewhere to hide.

"It's alright Butler," Brady says in a strange voice, "calm down, it's the chicks."

"Oh, yeah, yeah, the chicks, that's right." I stop myself from trying to hide underneath the coffee table but then I begin to walk around the house to explore my new environment.

I wander into the hallway and see four closed doors.

Two doors are to my right; they were my sister's room and mine. I look down the stretched hallway at the end, which seems three hundred feet longer than usual, and see the door to where my mom's room was. On the left side of the white hallway is a door to our bathroom. The blue carpet is being stretched up the sides of the wall. The doors of the hallway are doors to my mind.

Looking at the white wooden doors, I see golden doorknobs, which now look like little golden globes. I see my reflection on the doorknobs and realize that it is me on another golden planet. My mind begins to race pondering what my life is like in the other golden world.

I put my hand on the first door knob, which melts to my skin, and I twist it open. The door opens and I am invited into another realm. It is my room. My bed is hovering above the ground and the ceiling fan is swirling around like a propeller. I stand in the middle of the room and turn in all directions completely dazed by my new interactive atmosphere.

The patterns on the walls are forming faces. I see the faces of everyone who has ever walked into my room as if their presence was some how mystically trapped on my walls like paintings in a museum. I see myself in a mirror hanging on the wall, but I am no longer eighteen. I am six-years-old for a few seconds, then suddenly my face morphs to when I was ten, then it transforms again, this time I am sixteen. I recognize the **stare** on my face; it was the same lost **stare** I saw in the mirror the night my mom died when I didn't want to be the one staring back at myself anymore. Then my face melted like hot cheese on a pizza. I ran out of the room chased by terror.

"Brady!" I screamed running into the living room.

A blond girl was laying on his lap as he was petting her face, "What up Butler?"

"My face just melted!" I shouted on the brink of sanity.

He seemed unconcerned, "It's all right Butler, you're face didn't melt, it's just the acid," he says laughing.

I am about to argue the fact that my face really was melting off, but then I realized that he was right. It was the drug. My face was not melting. The other two guys sat on the couch, next to two other girls, staring at them. The girls seem strange, the shading of their faces began shifting and swirling. The living room feels awkward, so I return to the hallway.

Deciding that my room was too intense for me, I walk to my sister's door. I push the door open with my mind, and suddenly I am inside her world. Stuffed animals danced around on her bed. I am surrounded by singing toys.

I giggle.

The walls, sponge painted black and white, are fizzling around. The light in her room is dim, then it is bright, and then it changes to shades of red and purple. I look on her bed and see a red stuffed tickle me Elmo doll with huge eyes staring at me. My eyes widen as I realize that Elmo is my new best friend. I know this, because he tells me so. I grab the Elmo doll laughing a deep demented type of laugh and say, "Come on Elmo, you're hanging with me tonight."

With Elmo tucked safely under my arm, I leave Danielle's room gleefully. I close the door behind me, and then I turn to walk to my mother's old room. Placing my hand on the golden doorknob, my gleeful feelings of psychedelic bliss suddenly fall to sheer terror. I yank my hand off the knob; my eyes widen, as I realize that my mother is in the next room.

I run back into the living room and tell the guys with panicked concern, "Dude, we have to leave, my mom's here! Come on, we have to leave, we can't be doing this, let's go come on!"

"Butler, chill out," Brady said in an exhilarated tone of voice as he was overcome with blissful emotions induced by ecstasy, "you're just trippin'."

'Right, I'm just tripping,' I say reminding myself. The other people in the room glare at me, they are evil, they are aliens. I become afraid, and walk back into the hallway of safety.

I look down the hallway to my mother's room once again. Elmo's mouth is moving. He is talking. Only I understand what he is saying because he is my friend.

"Elmo, we have to go tell my mom not to die, okay?" I say looking into his egg shaped eyes. His mouth is moving. He agrees.

I creep carefully to her door again and I put my hand on the knob. Holding my breath, I open the door slowly and peek Elmo's head through the door like a telescope. I pull him back to my chest for safety, and then I interrogate him, "Was she there? What did you see?" I demand of him.

His mouth is moving. He tells me what he saw.

"Are you sure?" I ask him.

His oval eyes make it obvious that she is in there.

"Was she mad?" I ask him looking straight into his eyes to make sure he isn't lying to me. His red face stretched sideways and his eyes melted.

'Not a good sign,' I think to myself.

I slap him across the face and shout, "Damn it Elmo! Get a hold of yourself!" I demand. "Now is not the time to be cute. We have a mission to complete!"

Going into my mother's room has now become a self-imposed mission. I must confront her and I must talk to her.

Elmo and I retreat into my bathroom, which I instantly deem as our headquarters, and I lock the door. A huge mirror is a window into another portal. There is a man standing there staring at me. He is holding a red Elmo doll.

"Good thing you're here," I say to him, he says to me. Instantly we agree.

"Listen, my friend Elmo and I are on a mission, can you help?" I ask him, he asks me. Our universe must be parallel.

I nod my head, he nods his head, "I can help you," we say to each other.

We both place the Elmo doll next to the mirror so the two red creatures can discuss their game plan as we, the almighty generals of the universal realm, discuss our attack plan for accomplishing our unified mission of going into my/his mother's room.

"Listen," we speak at the same time, and I am overly impressed with our synchronized conversation. "My mom died, and I need to talk to her. She is in the other room where she died. How do you suggest my little red friend and I go about doing this?"

We both **stare** at the two red creatures contemplating their plans. We look into each other's eyes for trust. I see black pupils the size of dimes. He sees the same.

We discuss our plans telepathically so the people in the living room, the demonic aliens, can't invade and spoil our mission.

After an hour of intense telepathy and detailed planning, we both agree to walk up to the door and twist the knob. We will walk into her room and will go to her bedside where she will be, then we will talk to her and she will understand.

Yes…she will understand why I am on drugs.

Yes…she will understand that I am suffering from denial.

Yes…she will know these things because she is my mother and she will tell me that everything is okay.

I grab Elmo, "Come on, we have a mission to do," I say as the commanding general.

I saluted the guy in the mirrored parallel universe and wished him luck on his identical mission. He did the same.

Cracking open the door, I stick Elmo's head out and ask him if the coast is clear.

"John, what are you doing?" An alien voice and face appears from behind the door.

I slam it.

"Go away!" I shout. "Leave me alone, you can't take me to your planet!"

I hear the voice walking away mumbling that I am crazy.

Once again, I stick Elmo's head outside and he tells me to go. I creep out the door with huge slow steps sticking Elmo directly in front of me, just in case the aliens come back.

My mom's door is glowing. The golden knob is radiating. Unsure if the knob is radioactive, I place Elmo's mouth on the doorknob and make him open the door. I hear the aliens rumbling in the house, so I slip inside her room quickly and slam the door.

It is dark.

I flick on the light switch, and there she is...sitting on her bed. I look at Elmo and he grins. I smile victoriously.

With cautious steps, I creep over to her bed. She is staring at me. She is sitting in her velvet nightgown, silently staring into my soul with her water blue eyes.

"Hi mom," I say softly unsure if she is able to hear me.

She stands up. Then she walks over to a medical bed, which suddenly appears. She lies down in the bed.

She is staring at me. I try to speak, but I forgot what the man in the mirror told me to say.

"Um, mom," I say walking closer to her medical bed.

She **stares**.

I show her Elmo, hoping that he can get her to talk. It doesn't work.

"Hey, mom, I'm sorry I'm on drugs, but I need to talk to you," I say with a pleading voice. She **stare**s. "Um, I didn't want you to die mom," I tell her.

She **stare**s. I am walking closer to the bed.

"Are you mad at me, mom? I'm sorry I didn't cry mom. I love you. I'm sorry I'm on drugs mom. You're not mad, are you?" I ask, now at the foot of her bed.

She is moving her head on the pillow. Her leg is twitching that twitch. The same twitch that I had seen before.

"Mom!" I shout louder, "Don't die again!"

She is trying to say something, so I walk up closer to her face. I lean in and ask, "Mom, what is it you want to tell me?"

Her blue eyes **stare** into my black pupils, my face is inches away from hers, she begins to move her lips and she says...

"Butler!" Brady shouts running into the room.

My heart nearly exploded as he tackled me to the floor. I gasped for air.

"What the hell you doin', Butler, callin' us aliens," he said laughing, rubbing my head.

I couldn't speak. My delusional world had just been explosively interrupted and my brain is scrambling to comprehend.

I look to where my mom was, and there is nothing. My panicked eyes glare at Brady, he is smiling, as he is lost in his own psychedelic world.

"Where did she go?" I asked with a disbelieving voice.

Brady grabbed Elmo from me and laughed, "Where did who go? The girls are out in the living room, ya know, the ones you called aliens. Come on, let's go chill with the ladies."

"No, you don't understand, she was here." I state

emphatically on the verge of a nervous and mental breakdown.

"You're tripping Butler," he says rubbing the Elmo doll into my face.

I stand up and look around the room.

She is not there. She was not there.

I blink while I think of what just transpired. I looked at Brady as he pulled my arm so that I would follow him into the living room. We walked by a mirror in my mother's room and I **stare**d at it and realized, she was just a figment of my imagination.

My mother was dead, and so am I. The reality of life was falling apart like a broken ship out at sea…the darkness of my soul was now consuming me.

CHAPTER
TWENTY

"Dropping acid, dropping classes…"

A January fog filled the Bakersfield sky. Cal State Bakersfield had started, and already within the first week, I had dropped all my classes except for Screen Printing 101.

My nights consisted of smoking weed with my friends and selling Dickweed shirts. When I say sell, I mean I gave them shirts and they said they would pay me back, which of course, never happened.

Despite my disturbing incident with LSD a few weeks prior, I found myself doing more of it, with anyone else that was willing to take a plunge with me into the psychedelic world of the subconscious mind. When drugs are involved, it is amazing how many "friends" you can come across. I found myself with like-minded people who didn't want much out of life. People who were struggling with society's standards of survival; things like going to school and getting a job and doing something productive with their lives. So, instead, we did drugs.

Dave was getting frustrated with me and my lack of motivation to do something with my life.

"If you're going to live in my house, you need to get a job." He said one day as we met briefly in the hallway.

"I have a job," I told him, pointing to my Dickweed shirt.

He snickered cynically, "Dickweed is not a job, it's a hobby."

I took offense to his statement, and drove off somewhere to get stoned.

A few days later, while we were in the kitchen he asked with a tone of authority, "How's school going?"

I looked startled for a moment, "Um fine." I said stalling. "But I didn't like my classes, so I dropped them."

He scowled and crossed his arms, "You did what?"

"I dropped them."

"So you're not in school?" His voice radiated with irritation.

My body froze, as it always did with confrontation, as I tried to justify myself, "But I'm still taking Screen Printing 101," I said. "You know, so I can print my own shirts and save money on the costs and maximize the profits."

He shook his head and walked away. I took off in my truck and got stoned. Had he known that I was off smoking pot all the time, he would've kicked me in the ribs. At the time I figured I was making the right choices. I was hanging out with my friends selling shirts and smoking pot and tripping on LSD whenever possible. I didn't see the road I was headed down, but Dave did...

CHAPTER
TWENTY ONE

(A clean shaven step dad Dave in the desert)
"Hey Butler!"

One night in late January, I walked through the garage as Dave was working on his Harley. I needed something out of my truck when suddenly I stopped dead in my tracks.

"Hey Butler!" He shouted with direct anger. Right away I knew something was wrong. Dave never called me by my last name.

"When are you going to get a job?" He said sharply, wiping his hands with a rag.

Stunned and not knowing what to say to his abruptness, I just stood there and said with a shallow breath, "I've been, uh, looking."

"You've been looking for two months!" He said sharply.

"Well it's hard," I said, raising my hands weakly.

"So, let me get this straight. You don't have a job, you're not in school and you think you can come home at any hour of the night?"

I **stare**d at him; his tall and thin body squared off with mine in the driveway. The tension was thick.

"I'm sorry." I said, as a light misty rain came down through the darkness of the night.

He snickered stiffly, "Sorry isn't going to cut it, bud. You need to get your stuff and move out, right now!"

"Right now?" I asked shocked. I couldn't believe he was actually throwing me out.

"I've put up with this nonsense long enough, now get out!" He shouted, throwing the rag to the ground.

I **stare**d at him, unsure what to do, "Alright," I said weakly. Not wanting to agitate him further, I stood still.

He turned around without another word and went back to work on his motorcycle. I walked past him quietly feeling as though I'd been sucker punched in the stomach.

When I got into my room, I burst into tears. I was confused and had no idea what to do or where to go. I began boxing up my stuff with blurry eyes and loaded my belongings into my truck.

As I put the last of the things into my Dodge, I stood next to the door and said bye. Perhaps I said it too lightly, or perhaps he had had enough of me, but he just continued working on his Harley without even looking up.

I got into my truck and drove into the darkness of the night, and into the darkest time of my life.

CHAPTER
TWENTY TWO

(Adam Pierce #97 and John Butler #835 Bakersfield Fairground Supercross 1998)

"Slapping hands, knocking knuckles…"

"What happened to the grass?" I asked Brady as we walked across the lawn to the single story suburban house.

Brady chuckled, "I heard Pierce got a little crazy at the party the other night. I guess they were filming for a new video, so Pierce got on his dirt bike and started spinning donuts on the grass at like three in the morning. The cops came and everything, it was great."

I looked at the already dead grass and traced the dirt bike tire tracks with my eyes as we walked up to the front door and knocked. Someone peeked through a sheet covering the window. A few unlocking noises later, then the white door pulled open.

"What up guy?" A mellow voice emerged from a tall lanky fellow named Ferrell. He grinned at Brady while slapping his hand and knocking his knuckles in the standard "cool way" to greet people.

"What up, what up?" Brady answered with a question while walking through the door.

I followed him inside. I slapped Ferrell's hand and knocked his knuckles as well, you know, to make sure that I passed the coolness test.

"What up Bootler? I haven't seen you forever, where the hell have you been?" Ferrell asked closing the door. He pronounced my name like this every time.

I smirked and shrugged my shoulders, "I guess you could say I went to college...well, tried to anyway." Ferrell just bobbed his head in a nonchalant cool kind of way.

The three of us went into the living room to sit down. The walls were covered with posters of dirt bikes and hot chicks. There were three different colored couches, which were obviously found on the side of some road late at night.

All the couches formed a horseshoe around a black entertainment unit equipped with a large TV, Play Station and of course a 100-disk CD player with speakers big enough to blast away any neighbors' sleep within a few miles. A coffee table served as a cemetery for empty beer cans and dead cigarettes. The carpet, or what was left of it, had an interesting stain containing a peculiar mixture of puke, beer and piss.

"What's that stain from?" I asked naively looking at the pattern.

Ferrell smiled and said, "The question isn't what's that stain from, the better question is, who's that stain from?"

We launched into laughter.

We each sat on our own colored couch. Brady sat on a tan couch with stuffing spewing out the arms. Ferrell plopped himself down on a couch covered with sheets, while I sat next to a red haired guy named Todd, who of course, was passed out and slightly drooling on himself and breathing loudly.

"Is he okay?" I asked Ferrell while slightly nudging Todd in his ribs to make sure he wasn't in a coma.

Ferrell had resumed his focus on the video game he was playing and answered distantly, "Oh yeah, Drunk Todd is all good."

"Does he live here?" I asked.

"Nah, we just call him the guy on the couch like that movie Half Baked."

Brady and I smirked.

"Where's Pierce at?" Brady asked.

Ferrell **stare**d at the video game as if stuck in a trance, "I think he went to his brother's to use the phone, he'll be right back."

I **stare**d at the phone hanging on the wall, "What's wrong with that one?" I asked pointing.

Ferrell's eyes didn't move from the TV, "That phone, um, I guess you could say doesn't work?"

"Why is that?"

"Oh, you know, the Phone Company has a tendency to turn things off when your bill is $1,500." He said as if no big deal.

My eyes widened. His eyes narrowed on the TV screen while his thumbs danced on the controller.

"Too many 900 numbers, huh Ferrell?" Brady laughed.

"Twasn't me." Ferrell said with the mellowest voice you have ever heard. His voice was like the ocean; his words rolled like waves.

I liked Ferrell. He had the personality of water, always loose and ever flowing. He was a tall-lanky dirt bike rider and could have been the poster child for cool. Well, I guess, he *actually was* a poster child for cool, as I saw his new ad on the wall. The poster size ad featured him standing next to a gorgeous blonde girl wearing a pair of Dragon sunglasses with a photo of him doing a dirt bike trick. In my eyes, both Pierce and Ferrell were famous. They performed dirt bike tricks in front of thousands of fans and got paid for it. It was a dream job and was often televised on independent sport shows, as well as industry videos.

The house itself wasn't that old, but with a bunch of 21-year-olds partying every night, the house had seen better days. It was your typical bachelor pad, with a steady stream of stony-eyed-slackers flowing through at all hours of the day and night. Parties were like pimples; they popped up spontaneously and often ended in a mess.

We heard a car pull up followed by the sound of two doors being slammed shut. Some muffled voices, then the door sprang open.

A big burly guy with baby blue eyes and dented dimples wearing a flat-billed hat angled to the right came cruising in. Gafford was the third roommate of the house. He often acted as the mechanic, photographer and over all baby sitter of the two riders. He was the rock of the bunch, solid and stable. He too, was captain cool guy. In fact, 'guy' was the key word in the house. Instead of saying dude or bro, it was guy. And everybody said it, "guy."

"What up guy?" Gafford greeted with the G word, doing the same socially acceptable hand slap and knuckle knock to all of us.

"What up Gaff?" I said smiling, returning the slap to the hand and, of course, knocking the knuckles.

I'm cool. This is what I do. I slap skin and knock knuckles with other cool people. But what happens if I don't knock knuckles? Would I be failing the coolness part? Would that leave them hanging?

"Where the hell have you been Butler?" Gafford asked, pouring out fast food from a bag as he sat next to me, using the stretched out Drunk Todd as a backing. Todd slurped his spit in his sleep and grunted.

I picked up a french fry and said, "I went to live with my dad for awhile, but now I'm back."

"Sweet, sweet." Gaff said with a mouthful of fries.

Pierce had gone into his bedroom, but then returned to the living room with lighting like energy.

"What up guy?" Pierce said lovingly with a slap to the hand and, yes, once again, a knock to the knuckles. His neon-yellow dyed hair and electric blue eyes captured my attention.

"What up Pierce?" I said, receiving, yet again, another slap to the hand and knock to the knuckles. My hand was beginning to hurt. But I was being cool, so it didn't matter.

Pierce sat down and sandwiched me between himself and Gafford. Todd grunted once more.

Pierce put his arm around me like a big brother to a little brother, "So where've you been?"

I shrugged my shoulders slightly and smirked, "I went down to Corona Del Mar to live with my Dad and go to school. But I didn't like it down there."

"How the hell do you not like living near the beach?" He said, sounding like a live wire sticking out of a sink full of water. Pierce was always full of energy.

"Just wasn't my style," I said. "I guess my heart is in Bakersfield."

"Nah, it's just something in the water," Brady blurted.

Pierce laughed loudly and rubbed my head roughly, "So where you living now?" He asked.

"Good question," I said. "Dave kicked me out about two days ago. I'm staying with my friend Daniel in the meantime, but I need somewhere to live."

"No way," Pierce said in a thoughtful, fading outward kind of way. He sat silent for a second staring off into space, his knee bouncing like a basketball, then he smiled and looked at Ferrell and Gafford then spontaneously said, "I guess we've got a new roommate, boys."

"Really?" I asked, my voice was eager with excitement.

"Hell yeah, Butler. I can't have my little bro living out in the street now can I?" Pierce said with a twinkle in his eye.

Gafford munched his fries, "Yeah guy, you can stay here."

Ferrell bobbed his head in agreement.

"Thanks guys, I appreciate it."

"So what the hell are you waiting for? Get your crap and move already!" Pierce electrified the energy of the environment.

I looked at Brady with wide eyes and he laughed. We stood up and bolted out the door, into my truck and across town to Daniel's. I loaded up my stuff within thirty minutes, and was back to my new house. I couldn't have been more excited.

By the time I had finished unloading the boxes and organizing my stuff, a party had started in the living room. Pierce had a certain magnetic personality and it didn't take long for a crowd of people to congregate around him wherever he was. Pierce was like the pied piper, people flocked to him and he loved to entertain. His neon-yellow hair and spotlight personality dubbed him the nickname "The Highlighter" from a TV announcer. He was a raging sea in comparison to Ferrell's mellow pond.

I walked through the crowd of forty people in the living room, slapping hands and knocking knuckles with most of them, and made my way into the kitchen. The music was blaring and people were talking loudly. I had never partied in high school, being the clean cut racing kid from perfect suburbia, so the party life was new to me and it was exciting.

Drunk Todd had gotten off the couch because it was his wake up time-about five thirty in the evening-and he was eating breakfast, or rather he was drinking it: three beers through the tube of a beer bong.

He stood center stage in the middle of the kitchen in front of the sink stacked with dirty dishes from last month. He held the tube high in the air and then as if performing like a professional, he plunged it in his mouth and began to guzzle. I watched his cheeks bulge as the golden liquid gushed down with ungodly speed.

"Three seconds!" Gafford shouted while staring at a stopwatch.

"Three beers in three seconds?" I asked with amazement.

Todd belched like a barbarian.

He was your typical Irishman. Red hair, fudge brown eyes, covered with freckles and always drunk. He was also the undisputed beer bong champion of the house and was more than eager to defend his title.

"Come on guy, you're next. You gotta hold your own in this house." Todd said sloppily, wiping beer foam from his mouth with the back of his hand.

I looked at the other guys in the kitchen. The eagerness in their eyes encouraged my excitement.

Todd handed me the tube and told me to plug it with my thumb. Then he curved the tube around and angled the funnel sideways as he poured in three beers. He poured them perfectly making sure there wasn't too much foam or any air pockets.

"Alright guy," he said. "Just put the tube in your mouth, and when you're ready just chug it."

"Come on Bootler, you can do it!" Ferrell cheered casually as he raised a beer can in the air as a sign of support.

Pierce let out what I called the Spanish Siren, a scream that sounded like a strung out hyena, "Yeah guy! IE YAY AY HI YEI!"

I put the tube to my mouth as Todd raised the funnel high in the air. Then, without a worry in the world, I removed my thumb and got a wave of cold beer down my throat. Gafford held the stopwatch. It seemed to take forever as I watched the river of alcohol drain through the tube.

I couldn't control my breathing and gagged on the beer, forcing Budweiser through my nose. My eyes watered and they all laughed hysterically. Pierce let out another Spanish Siren, and Gafford shouted, "10 seconds!"

Todd raised his arms in victory and shouted like an Irish warrior, "Still the champ!" Then he grabbed my head, **stare**d me in the eyes and screamed, "YEAH GUY!"

Then, Drunk Todd head butted me.

Yes, that's right; Drunk Todd hammered his head against mine.

It felt like I had been smacked by a two by four. I stumbled past my new roommates-each of them patting me on the back, slapping my hand, knocking my knuckles-and out the kitchen into the swarm of strangers.

I was instantly buzzed from the beer bong and my head hurt. I walked through the crowded living room, this time avoiding any hand slapping or knuckle knocking, and wobbled in front of the couch where a bunch of hot chicks were sitting. The mad rush of beer made me burp up foam. The girls **stare**d at me and laughed. I waved, wobbled some more, then puked behind the couch.

My contribution to the carpet had now been made.

CHAPTER
TWENTY THREE

"*Crashing Down...*"

The walls are wavy, but they feel good. My stomach is turning over and over, and suddenly I am in a different realm...

The two pills I took about forty five minutes earlier are now rolling through my veins. Brady's green punk rocker spiked hair is swiveling around like small snakes in the grass.

We are laughing.

We are rolling.

We are escaping...

We are on ecstasy.

I had left Pierce's house after he and Ferrell had their falling out, and the house was being repossessed by Pierce's dad because none of us could pay rent or the bills for that matter.

So now, I have moved to Brady's parent's house and am sleeping on his floor. My money was gone but somehow, we'd find enough money to buy drugs.

I was now officially a loser. My life was lacking any significance or meaning.

Brady and I would do ecstasy almost every night, and each morning after a psychedelic binge, I'd wake up half dead. My body ached, my mind was melted with mixed memories, and I was continuing to be buried beneath the deadly hand of drug induced depression and denial.

Eventually Brady and I got sick of each other, so I was off to another house, where I'd do the same stupid stuff, and then off to another house, to someone else who would agree to let me sleep on their floor as long as I promised to "better myself."

Better myself? Did that mean doing more drugs? That's the way I interpreted it.

By the time I was 19, only a year after beginning my journey through the lost land of psychedelics, I had done over 50 hits of acid, ecstasy and mushrooms and moved to ten different houses. My brain was burnt out, and so was my soul. I kept running from my problems, and yet they always seemed to be waiting for me when I came down from my highs. As they say, what goes up, must come crashing down.

CHAPTER
TWENTY FOUR

"*Chasing Butterflies...*"

I stood next to the door and whispered goodbye. I knew it'd be the last time that I'd see her.

In the dark room, her body looked as though it was already dead, but with the slow heaving motion of her chest, I knew that she was just barely hanging on.

What happened to all those years that I had seen her in her room watching TV, sitting upright, and drinking a diet soda from a plastic cup? What happened to those times in which I would go to her room before I went to bed and kissed her goodnight? What happened to…what happened to all those things that seemed so innocent, and now they were gone forever?

I don't know much about death except the fact that I have experienced it second hand. I've watched my grandfather die, my grandmother die, a few friends, but nothing absorbed me as much as watching my mother die. From the outside looking in, I could stand near the doorway of her room and watch her from a thousand miles away. This wasn't really her and she really wasn't dying.

There she is, right there. In bed, eyes closed, slowly breathing a handful of breaths before she stops breathing all together. What is she thinking about? Is she scared? Does she know that she is dying? Surely she must know that she is dying. How could she not?

Is she worried about dying? Will she go to heaven? Does she even care? Will God take one look at her and deem her unworthy? What is death and why does it happen?

I don't know these answers, but I do know that my mother is dying. She has fought the battle of cancer, and the cancer has won. She has lost. And not only has she lost as if losing a game of cards in which she could have another turn at playing, she is losing for real this time and certainly she will never have another chance to play.

If I could, I would step into her body and say softly, "It's okay, mom. I'm going to die for you. You can be me and I'll be you…I'll die for you….don't be scared, I can do this so you don't have to."

As I think of these thoughts, I am now 18 and sitting in my room alone with a bag full psychedelic mushrooms, a six pack and a smoldering bong full of smoke. There are nearly 20 people crammed into my apartment, guys and girls groping each other on ecstasy. But I don't want anything to do with them. I want my mother.

The mushrooms start to take effect and I am soon seeing my room as my mother's room. I pace around and mumble things to myself, things like, *'Don't die, not yet, don't die, I'll die, you don't have to die, I'll die for you.'*

I hear some girls rolling around the apartment outside my room giddy with joy and laughter. But I'm not laughing. I'm fucked up and I'm high, but I'm not laughing. In my mind I see my mother on my bed. She is dying. She is not laughing. She is sleeping taking her last few breaths. *Don't die mom, not yet...let me die for you.*

As I say this, she breaths slowly and painfully. She is on my bed, but she is not on my bed. The mushrooms are working.

I want to think and analyze her death, so in my psychedelic induced mind, she will not die. She has been resurrected by my drug reasoned mind, and maybe, just maybe, I can save her, unlike the first time in which I couldn't.

I walk over to the bed were she is sleeping and suddenly she vanishes. The mushrooms come in waves, and in this relapse of illusion, I begin to panic. I open a beer, eat a handful of mushrooms, pop some ecstasy, and smoke a bowl.

She reappears.

"No, John," she says, "Don't do this."

"But I need you, mom. I need you. Please don't die."

She looks at me, and although it is just my pillow that is looking at me, I believe that she is telling me that I can save her. I drink another beer, smoke another bowl, munch on some more mushrooms, and suddenly the room becomes a forest.

There are trees. Trees so tall that I can't see the sunshine. I am running through the trees trying to find her again. Birds are flying around. They are trying to fly through my face but I swat them away. I look down at my blue carpet and notice that I am standing in the middle of the ocean, and I begin to sink.

"Mom!" I shout. "Mom, don't die! Don't leave me!" I obviously shout this loud enough to have my roommate come in.

"John?" He says knocking while opening the door. Gary is a big guy that is my roommate and doubles as an overall protector. "Are you okay? Everybody heard you screaming. What's going on?"

His mere appearance frightens me, so I lock myself in my closet. He is the epitome of death, because I can't find my mother, so I associate his appearance as the ending of my mother's life.

"Go away!" I shout from the corner of my locked closet. I hear him mumble something, but I can't discern English anymore. Everything is coming through in waves.

In my closet, I see my clothes all hanging from hangers. And because I am sitting crammed against the corner, this view gives me the perception that all of these clothes are actually people standing over me. Faceless fashions, looking down on me, despising me because of her death.

"I didn't want her to die!" I sob to the nearest sweatshirt. The hood looms over me and tells me that I am crazy.

"Where is she? Where did she go?" I ask the pile of shoes strewn across the floor.

They don't respond, they just sit there.

After an hour of yelling at my clothes, I crack open the door and make sure the dark figure of death isn't standing outside. I see my bed and nothing more. The coast is clear.

I walk out my closet and notice that the cans of beer have all been drank. Did I drink them all? I don't remember. Perhaps I had a black out with all the drugs that I'm on, but I don't remember drinking the beer. Perhaps death had drunk all of my beer. That bastard. Not only did he take my mother, he took my beer as well.

Never mind the beer. I have a bottle of Nyquil in my medicine cabinet. I open it up and drink the full bottle. I like this feeling because I know that I will soon be drunk with a depressant and I will be able to sleep.

Beer, mushroom, weed, ecstasy and a full bottle of Nyquil. Yes. I can finally find my comfort zone and sleep off this illusion. But it won't stop. It keeps coming.

My walls are now rocks of a cave. I am sitting in the middle of my room scared to sleep in my bed because I associate my bed with being a coffin in which my mother has been buried in. There are faceless cavemen cruising around my room looking for a dinosaur to kill. I tell them to leave but they just ignore me and look for things to kill.

My roommate pops his head in through the door and his head is ten feet tall. Nothing but a face and a jaw that hangs to the ground. His voice comes through in a slow morphed motion of incomprehensible waves, "jOhn….aRe…yOU…oKAy?"

I throw an empty beer can at his face and suddenly he disappears. I don't know if he really appeared or if I had just in fact thrown an empty beer can at the undeserving door.

I look back to my bed and my mom is there again. She is sitting up and fixing her hair.

"Mom! You're okay?" I say.

She says, "Yes, I am. But you're not. You need help."

"What do you mean?" I say, feeling nauseated.

"Stop what you're doing. Just stop it!" She screams at me. She is angry and she is livid. She takes a beer can and throws it at me.

"But mom!" I scream, "I told you I would die for you, isn't that enough!"

She suddenly grows wings and flies around the room. She is slowly becoming a butterfly, a butterfly I cannot catch.

I now vomit on myself and she is repulsed. She is yelling at me telling me that I am a drug addict. Didn't she know that I did this for her? Yes, I did this for her, because if I take enough drugs, I will die and I will take her place and she will become immortal through her son's death. Yes, I am Jesus. I have taken away all of her sins and I will give her eternal life through my sacrifice of death.

I look at the vomit on my clothes and I peel them off. Apparently when I was in the closet, I had put on six layers of clothes, so the first layer doesn't really matter. I have emerged from my vomit covered cocoon and I am now a butterfly. I will chase her and I will catch her. I will grab her by the wings and tell her not to die.

She will listen to me because I have overcome her. I will be triumphant and she will live and I will die. The problem will be solved.

As I stand to take flight, the room suddenly becomes my room. She is not there because she was never there. The mushrooms, weed, ecstasy, beers and Nyquil have betrayed me. They are nothing more than a substance leading to delusion.

I stand to look around and I see my face in the mirror. My pupils are different. One is the size of a pin drop, the other the size of a dime. I am whacked out of my mind and I want to die.

My bed is empty. I am empty. I want to die but I am still alive. This sucks. Not only have I failed at life, but I have failed at death as well.

I crawl into my bed and wish I could take my mother's place. But all I get is a hangover and a sense of dread in the morning.

I offered to die for her, and she flew away. My addiction was nothing more than just that…an addiction. I was slowly dying, just like I had wanted, but death seemed to leave me behind in this thing called a fucked up life.

I never thought I'd be a drug addict trapped in a room chasing after my mother, but this is what my life had become at 18. I wanted to die, but all I could do…was live.

CHAPTER
TWENTY FIVE

"*Rolling Through the Valley of Death…*"

My body was hollow. The pain had been the same two years prior that exact morning.

I sat next to my mother's grave and watched the morning haze glisten in the sun rising above the eastern San Joaquin mountaintops.

"Are you okay?" A voice vaguely rang out from across the cemetery.

I looked over and saw Jeremy walking from his uncle's grave. I could tell that he had been crying. His face flushed with a blank **stare**, accompanied by glossy red eyes.

"Yeah. I'm fine," I said without another word.

He must have known by the look on my face to let me have a few more minutes to myself.

I looked back down at my mother's grave. ***"Karen Lynn Donnelly-Beloved Wife and Mother"*** the cold tombstone read, containing so little words, for such an outspoken life. Is this what life was all about?

I closed my eyes one last time and took in a deep breath. The silence of the deep breath penetrated the darkest corners of my soul.

My body felt weak after I stood up too quickly. I took a step back then regained my balance. Jeremy came up again and asked, "Are you okay?"

I nodded.

We gathered back into Nathan's car without a sound and left the cemetery. It was obvious that we were all contemplating our same question of existence. As detached as we were, we still had to focus on finding Gary.

The night before I had been working at Video City in Rosedale. My roommates Gary and Izzy came by before I was scheduled off and said they were going to Mike's house for an "adventure."

I felt apprehensive about letting Gary go on his own "adventure" without me. I had always been there, and I knew that he used me as his psychological anchor when the storms got rough. They could tell that I wasn't enthusiastic about the idea, but I knew they'd do it anyway so I agreed to meet them at Mike's house when I got off work.

When I arrived the atmosphere felt abnormal right off the bat. I walked up to Mike's back porch and saw Gary rocking back and forth on the staircase beneath a flickering light bulb, wearing a white and blue beanie topped off by his trademark cowboy hat. It was nearly 100 degrees the night of June fourth, and Gary was a 270-pound beanie-wearing cowboy sweating profusely.

I rushed to his side.

"Are you okay, Gary?" I looked into his eyes.

His quarter size pupils looked right past me and I knew that he was gone. I called out for Izzy. He and Mike came out wide-eyed and giggling through the sliding glass door.

I asked them, "What happened, is he okay?"

"Yeah, dude he's fine. He's rolling," they giggled.

I obviously knew he was on ecstasy but I didn't know how much he had taken. I had never seen him in such a desolate state of blankness. He just sat there rocking back and forth with a huge childish like grin on his face staring off into nothing; completely oblivious to everything but the drug that was running through his veins.

I followed Izzy and Mike through his house and into his black lit room. Multi-colored neon posters accented the walls, as a Pink Floyd video playing on the television dazzled the small room in brilliant spouts of light. "Here John, I got two left," Mike said enthusiastically handing me two aspirin sized pills.

I felt disturbed by the look of eagerness in their amplified eyes and the scene that I had just encountered outside with Gary. I felt a tightness of resistance in my chest as I took the two pills out of Mike's hand. My mind was racing a thousand miles an hour of ways to justify doing the drug. I had been the one that got Gary into drugs, and I felt a certain obligation to be right next to him psychologically, so we could encounter the metaphysically cosmic journey of psycho phenomena together. Needless to say, I popped the two pills and waited for my journey to begin.

Perhaps it was the saturated atmosphere of psychedelics or anxiety of mental expansion, but the pills took full effect within five minutes of ingestion. The brightness of the posters on the wall now had a new illuminating presence. My hands were becoming overly sensitive to the touch, and the feeling of being internally uplifted was compelling enough to stand up and start exploring my new psychoactive environment, a place of psychotherapy that I had familiarized myself with all too often in the preceding six months.

The rolling sensation often referred to by users is like a lopsided wheel of feelings within your solar plexus. At the height of the drug, the lopsided wheel seems to feel more on the upswing of pure overwhelming sensations, as opposed to the down of the trip, which feels like a winding down of the soul from the heavens.

With dilated pupils and heightened intuition, I began to look for Gary. I found him sitting on the tailgate of his big old Chevy looking up at the stars. I walked up to him and sat down without saying a word.

I could tell that he was still at the peak of his psychedelic experience as I began to guide him.

"What are you thinking about?" I asked.

He paused for a moment. His eyes still focused on the stars.

Then without looking at me asked, "What is this place?"

I could tell he was referring to the vastness of his mind as evident by the look of immense fascination as he **stare**d at the boundless universe above. Gary and I had done ecstasy a few times before then, however, this time it was different. Before, Gary had just experienced the physical sensations of the drug. However this time he had delved into the bottomless pit of his subconscious mind with the aid of the psychedelic. Ecstasy trips are always different. Some times they are physical, though this one seemed to contain a lot of acidic properties as found in LSD. Having experienced this vastness myself many times over the past few months, I knew how to guide him through his mind.

"Look at the universe, Gary. What do you see?"

He responded vaguely, "Swirling stars."

"What do those stars represent?" I questioned.

"My thoughts," he answered with a fading tone.

"Your mind is like the universe, and the stars are your thoughts," I continued, "what you think about gives light to the darkest night's sky."

His eyes widened as he pondered this thought.

"Look at the darkness of the moon...it represents your subconscious mind. The brightness of the sun represents your conscious mind. These two things are the balance of life."

He continued staring off into the black abyss for several minutes. His thoughts came through in waves.

"What else are you thinking about?"

"Christie," he said with a smile.

Christie was Izzy's cousin. Gary had fallen head over heels for any girl that came to the apartment and she was his latest interest. She on the other hand had every other guy in mind besides Gary. Gary continually tried to pursue her romantically but she wasn't interested. She had called him earlier that night and said that she was going out to party with some of her friends. This quickly became a negative blip on his emotional radar. He began to dwell on her being out with other people. His mind quickly began to fixate on Christie. Disaster was coming quickly.

"Where is she at?" He began to panic.

At this point I knew that he'd either come crashing down from his psychedelic high, or I could try to salvage his failing emotions by convincing him that he could still be with her intuitively through the metaphysical realm of reality.

"It's okay, buddy, take a deep breath," I said in an attempt to calm him down.

He began to ramble on, "What if she's getting drunk with other guys, What if..."?

"Gary, it's alright, just close your eyes and picture her face."

With hesitation he closed his eyes and listened to what I was saying.

"Picture yourself right next to her where ever she is at."

I was trying to make him believe that he could communicate with her through his subconscious mind. I knew that psychedelics increased his sensations, and by explaining to him that he was still with her, although he wasn't, was my best attempt to keep him from falling into emotional calamity. Psychedelics can cause you to dwell on things to such a point where you actually believe that life isn't worth living anymore.

After a few minutes I had him talking to her as if she were really there. He was having an imaginary conversation with her. But just when things had gotten calmed down, we heard a blood curdling scream echo throughout the neighborhood, "Gary!"

Everything fell apart.

Gary jumped off the truck and went running down the dark alley in search of Christie shouting out her name. Everything was psychotic. Christie was at a party a few blocks away and she was walking back wasted drunk. Gary went running up to her.

Gary's mind was twisted back sideways with concern for Christie but she was just jabbering on about the guys at the other party with absolutely no regard for what Gary had just been through. She was acting sloppy as she walked into the house and completely blew off Gary. This absolutely crushed his whole world. He was devastated. It was a deep stab to the heart of love. I was intuitively on the same wavelength and I could tell he was over it…he was going to kill himself.

Gary stormed off to his truck and I followed him.

"Gary wait..."

"No! I'm leaving!" He shouted in psychedelic panic.

He jumped into his truck and started it up. I ran up to his window and tried to talk him out of it, but he just sped off in his big old truck and didn't look back.

Now my head was twisted back sideways. Mike and Izzy were freaking out as well because now they had something to dwell on. Everyone was upset. We all decided to split up and go find him. Mike and Izzy took off in his car, and I took off with the other two guys there, Jeremy and Nathan.

It was about four in the morning and we were driving around the streets looking for Gary. Somehow we got off track and we went down Round Mountain Rd. We were listening to the ocean on the radio which made the car seem like a ship. Our minds had wondered off in psychedelic confusion. We just had a lingering question on our minds, "Where is he?" It echoed on and on, "Where is He?"

As time went on we had made our way over to Hillcrest cemetery. By now the question of "Where is hc" went to "Where is He?" As in where is God? It quickly developed into a spiritual quest for reason.

I had once again put myself in a position facing life and death questions. How was I going to tell his parents? I felt horrible. I was desperately seeking something deeper. God had sent me on a spiritual journey through the flames of hell. I had walked through the valley of the shadow of death once again.

We pulled into the cemetery and the three of us split up. I went directly to my mother's grave and broke down crying. My life had once again fallen to the gutter. Through my tears I read the tombstone, *"January 14, 1960-June 5, 1998"* That's when it occurred to me that it was exactly two years ago that morning when my mother had died.

Painful memories began flashing before my eyes. All I could remember was the **stare** on my mother's face the morning she died. My body once again felt numb and hollow. As my memories and tears drizzled away, I once

again had a pounding answer echoing in my head,
"Everything happens for a reason…everything happens for a reason…Everything happens for a reason."

CHAPTER
TWENTY SIX

(Me the morning after…this picture is a good reason not to do drugs.)
"Long Ride Home…"

The ride home from the cemetery was long and dreadful. In my mind I kept going over what I was going to say to Gary's parents and everybody else. I thought for sure that he was dead, and I felt responsible. Just like the morning two years prior, I was in a zone of contemplation. I was thinking about my existence. What was it and why was I here?

When we pulled into the parking lot of the apartments at Whispering Meadows, we were relieved to see Gary's big white truck parked in his usual spot. Anxiously, we all rushed into the apartment to see what had happened to him.

As we walked through the door we saw Izzy sleeping on the couch and Mike lying on the floor. I walked into Gary's room and saw that he was asleep peacefully as well. The lion's den was calm, and I the lion was at ease.

Later in the afternoon when everyone woke up, we all discussed what had transpired the night before. Gary said that he had been crushed by Christie's actions and he wanted to kill himself. He said that he took off and was driving around in tears. As he crossed the railroad tracks near Roberts lane and Olive, he said that he stopped and waited for the inevitable impact from a train that was less than a mile down the track. He told us that as he waited, he prayed.

As he shared this story with us, we felt an overwhelming peace since we knew what the prayer had obviously accomplished. Gary said that as the train approached, the spirit, or an angel perhaps, touched him and he drove off the tracks of death and back onto the road of life. Thus he avoided death by a speeding train, and retained his right to live.

After this experience our drug use in the apartment temporarily dwindled down for a few weeks. The emotional scar of this tragedy was still fresh in our minds. But as time went on, and people came and went, the drugs were back and our minds were back on the same reckless track.

As August rolled around, the three of us had drifted apart. Gary and Izzy began getting irritated with each other since they had to share a room together. The only time we were all happy together is when we were all on some kind of substance; whether it was drugs or alcohol. The ecstasy that we had taken changed a lot of our views and perceptions about life. Personally it sent me down a road of self-discovery.

Within the past two years I had gone from an honors student who was on a successful track to Cal State Fullerton, to a drug addict in Oildale. I thought it was quite ironic. The night my mother died I remember feeling enraged because as I put it, "There were so many drug addicts in Oildale that deserved to die, and yet He was taking my mother." Now I was the drug addict in Oildale. Did I deserve to die? Perhaps. But I didn't, and now I was on a mission to find out why I had survived.

Someone once told me that life is like a hallway and the doors you choose to go through are your choice. Those choices all had consequences and benefits. It was quite clear to me that the choices I had made; dropping out of Fullerton, leaving Corona Del Mar, moving in with my "bros", not listening to Dave, had brought me to my present situation. I carefully analyzed every little decision that I had made and it occurred to me that they had taken me nowhere. But it also dawned on me that I could still make decisions regarding my future.

I was now at the point of deciding, do I stay in the apartment and further ruin myself, or do I make a decision to move and start all over again? I decided to pray and wait for the answer. Sure enough, it came in the most unusual coincidental way.

CHAPTER
TWENTY SEVEN

(Bob Swanson in classic form)

"A Spiritual Intervention…"

After my 19th birthday, I called up my old friend Bob Swanson, a good righteous man of about fifty years old, with a strong foundation of Christian faith. He was a classic character; tall, thin, peppered gray hair, who always wore a button up shirt with his glasses tucked in the pocket, brown loafer shoes and denim jeans with a big belt buckle that said 'BOB.'

We sat down together in my apartment and he **stare**d at me with his honest blue eyes.

"So," he said looking around at the empty beer boxes lining the apartment, "what's going on in John Butler's life?"

My soul stumbled over my stomach as my eyes began to tear up.

"I need to get out of this," I said.

"Out of what?"

I looked around at all the destruction and chaos of the apartment which resembled my life and lifted up my hands, "All this."

"So what are you going to do about it?"

I **stare**d at the ground and nodded numbly, shrugging my shoulders stupidly.

"I don't know. I don't know what to do anymore."

He took a deep breath, perhaps unsure of what he was about to commit to.

"Well, how about you move in with me and my family?"

I **stare**d into his blue eyes. He **stare**d into my suffering soul.

"Are you sure?" I asked.

"Yes, but you need to make some changes."

"Yes, yes, anything," I said desperately.

"No drinking, no drugs, no coming home late…and you need to find a job," he said firmly, his eyes still locked onto mine.

Inside I gasped at what he was proposing, perhaps feeling scared that it was going to be too much to commit to, but I was desperate and I had nowhere else to go and no one else to turn to.

I thought deeply for a moment. The past year of my life had been one wild party and it was certainly taking its toll on my life, my body and my soul. Bob was a respectable devoted man. His mere presence brought a godly comfort and hope.

So, I agreed.

"Alright," I said softly.

He smiled.

I smiled even brighter, feeling for once in the past year, that I was making the right decision.

Then he looked again at the beer boxes and thrashed apartment and said, "Mind if we pray?"

"Absolutely."

We bowed our heads as he began, "Heavenly Father, I want to thank you for this friendship. Lord I ask that you guide John as he makes these steps closer to you. Father I ask that you show him Your plan for his life, and that he will have the courage to walk with you. I thank you for getting John through this time of life, and I ask that you are with him as he begins this new chapter of his life. In Jesus name we pray."

And together, we said, "Amen."

My eyes opened up to meet Bob's heavenly blue **stare** of honesty and trust.

"Thanks Bob," I said. "I needed that."

He smiled, "We all need it."

And with that, I began a new chapter in my life...

CHAPTER
TWENTY EIGHT

"Some things never change…"

When I moved into Bob's house with his wife and son who was my age, I was determined to do better.

I got a job selling cell phones at a local grocery store and began reading the Bible.

"God has a plan for your life," Bob would tell me.

"Well I sure wish he'd tell me, because I don't want to be slinging cell phones forever," I said.

He smiled and asked, "What do you want?"

My eyes focused as I **stare**d into the unseen future and said, "I want to be a millionaire. I want to sell Dickweed worldwide and make a fortune. Then I want to buy a mansion, which I'll call the 'Dickweed Palace' and I want a fleet of dirt bikes and cars and trucks and I want a really hot wife."

He took in my self-absorbed wants for my future and thought for a long moment. Bob was a listener and I was a talker. He was always asking me simple questions, which I would then talk about for five minutes before winding back around to the original question. He was guiding me.

"It sounds like you *want* a lot of stuff," Bob said wisely, "But what does God *want* for your life?"

I looked at him stupidly and shrugged my shoulders, "I don't know. What?"

He took a deep breath while holding the Bible in the palm of his hand, then his eyes narrowed into my soul. "What God wants from John Butler, is for John to give him his life. God has created you with your many talents and gifts and he wants you to use those for Him. When you try to obtain these things that the world tells you you should *want*, you end up wasting your life chasing after the wind. Cars will break down, houses can crumble, and money and women will come and go. But it's the things that you do for God that last for an eternity."

I **stare**d at him and thought. "Hmm, good answer."

He smiled his wide white smile, "It's not just a good answer, it's the truth. This book," he said holding up his brown Bible, "this book has the truth for your life."

I looked down at my borrowed Bible from his bookshelf and thought about what he was saying. Part of me wanted to go back to my old life of beer and bongs, and yet, another part of me wanted something more; like become a missionary, or a priest, or a monk, anything but a stoner and a drunk.

He closed his Bible, as I did mine.

"God has a plan for you, kid."

"I hope so," I said.

He smiled confidently and I smirked.

"Good night," he said. "I love you."

"I love you too, Bob."

Then I went into my room and drank a bottle of beer buried behind some boxes in the closet.

Damn it…I guess some things never change.

CHAPTER
TWENTY NINE

"Triumphs and trials…"

I am standing on a suburban sprawl of grass beneath the sunny September sky. A year before I was living in Corona Del Mar, struggling with myself, denying my mother's death, resisting change and trying to get a college education at Cal State Fullerton.

And now, I am living in a conservative Christian home, reading a Bible, and trying to change all that I had become in the past 365 days. Amazing how much a year's difference can make.

But what was I going to do now? Where was I going? What am I doing? Who, what, when, where, why, how…so many questions, so little answers. Perhaps it was the year's worth of psychedelics, or just the fact that I was a wandering and wondering 19 year old, but now, that is all I seemed to do was ask questions.

Life with Bob was comfortable. He was consistent, unlike me, and he was honest, unlike me. Bob had led a holy life, never drinking a drop of alcohol, *definitely* unlike me. I believe that he was sent into my life as a guide, a counselor or perhaps an angel. God definitely had a sense of humor to pair the two of us together. But, as much as I tried to adapt, those flesh born faults kept calling me back to my old habits.

They say when you have a triumph you are met by trials. Bob had illustrated that after Jesus' baptism, He was tempted by the devil in the desert for forty days. I had prayed the sinner's prayer with Bob, wanting and willing for God to do something better with my life, and sure enough, the devil came searching for me.

One day while wandering the web, I got an e-mail from a guy that had heard about Dickweed and that he wanted to get together to talk about other business stuff.

I had him come over to Bob's conservative castle, and it didn't take long before the two of us began talking about acid and drugs.

"Yeah, man, I was frying balls last night," Zack said with a devilish grin.

"Really? I bet that was fun...I haven't fried in a few months since living here."

He put his hand in his pocket and pulled out some strips of paper, "Here, you can have these. They're strong."

I looked at his palm at the purple strips of paper. My soul said no, but my flesh said yes. I noticed that the door to my room was open, but I didn't think too much of it because I thought that I was home alone.

"Thanks dude," I said stealing the sinful strips from his hand. I wasn't sure if I was going to do them, but just knowing that I had them in my possession made me feel powerful, as if I could plunge into the psychedelic palace of my mind at any time.

About an hour later, I left with another friend of mine named Jason. We were out cruising around town when I got an urgent page on my pager from Bob's work number. Thinking that something was wrong, I pulled over to the nearest phone and called him.

"What's up Bob?" I asked being chirpy.

He hesitated, "What are you doing, John?"

"Just out running errands with Jason."

He hesitated again, which wasn't like Bob, since he was always full of the spirit and eager to engage into conversation at all times, "I just got a phone call from Joel," he said referring to his straight as an arrow son who happened to be training to become a sheriff.

"Oh yeah," I said weaker, my heart began hammering as I began to realize what had happened.

"He said something about drugs being in the house...is this true?" The hurt in Bob's voice was hardening into disappointment.

I took a shallow breath, replaying the act of my transgression throughout my thoughts. *Why did I take drugs from a guy that I had never met before? Why did I bring them into Bob's house? Why did I leave my door open? Why was Joel listening to us outside the door? Why, oh, why, oh, why?!*

Bob's honest voice asked me again as I stood silent on the other end of the phone, "Is this true, John?" I knew that he wanted the truth, but I could also hear in his voice that he didn't want it to be true.

I sighed, "Yes, Bob, it's true."

He let out the deepest breath of disappointment and discouragement that I have ever heard. That alone said it all. I was crushed and angry with myself.

"Well, when you get home, we need to talk."

Oh, the worst situation that I could possibly face. I hate confrontation. I dreaded it. This couldn't be happening because it shouldn't be happening. Why was I so stupid!

"Okay," I said.

Then we hung up, and I walked back to Jason's truck and sat down sadly in the passenger seat.

"What do you want to do now?" Jason asked.

My mind meandered for a moment, and then I put my hand in my pocket and pulled out the purple psychedelic papers. In that moment I had a choice; I could make the right choice and throw the paper out the window, or I could put the paper in my mouth and melt away and hide within the mountains of my mind...

I looked at Jason as he looked at me. Then I handed him the other piece of purple paper and I smiled, sinfully, sadly.

Then we went to his friends house and spent the night sizzling away in a world so fake, so lonely, so made of psychedelic plastic that you just wanted to burn it all down and look at the melted remains. All of this just so you would know, that every wrong thing in life was truly death, and that every wrong choice we could ever make, would just be another fork in the path of life which would eventually lead to death.

Life...life...life...oh how deadly it was.

CHAPTER
THIRTY

(Dickweed and Durden, January 2001)

"Ways of the Wicked…"

Fast forward through me leaving Bob's house and moving my stuff while he wasn't there…so I wouldn't have to face confrontation…so I wouldn't have to face my dark demons of addiction…so I wouldn't have to face Bob and see that look of broken hope in his eyes.

Now fast forward through six more months of the same stupid stuff. The calendar pages flip from September, through December and land somewhere in the wild winds of April.

There I am living on people's couches…there I am watching walls watering down like waterfalls into psychedelic puddles of emptiness…there I am staring at the sky seeing it sizzle into an open void of colorful nothingness.

I remember sitting inside a skate board shop in down town Bakersfield on Chester Avenue. I don't know anything about skateboards, but by a chance encounter selling Dickweed shirts to a business owner named Tyson, I had gotten a job as the shop manager.

"I'm looking for somebody to run the shop," Tyson said.

My ambitious excitement and over active imagination chimed in. I figured I could use some creative marketing ideas and make the shop a huge success, and of course, as a result, would become rich.

Tyson owned an oil service company and the skateboard shop was a side investment, or better, just a tax write off. He was in his late 30's, short and stocky, with a wife and two kids.

Although he had been married for the past twenty years, he preferred running around the downtown bar scene with his 21 year old secretaries. He had a lot of money and liked to use it as a sociable service to young girls who wanted a sugar daddy.

"I need somebody to run this shop and make a profit," he said as I sat next to a box of Dickweed shirts, which he was buying for eight hundred bucks.

I smiled my salesman smile and said, "I can do that."

His wide and wild devilish denim blue eyes looked me over, "Good. Here are the keys."

And as easy as that, I had full authority of the skate shop. What seemed like an easy dream come true, would soon become a hellish nightmare…

At the time, in early April 2001, I had been staying with a guy named Tommy, but since I didn't have a job and didn't pay him any rent for the past six months, he had given me a week to move out.

"I need a place to stay," I told Tyson, hoping I could get him to hook me up with an apartment or a house.

He crossed his thick arms and **stare**d at the beautiful blonde girl who was his pick of the day. I thought he was thinking of a solution to my housing dilemma, but as I caught him winking and puckering his lips at the girl, I realized that he was just undressing her in his mind.

"Tyson?!" I said trying to get his attention.

"What?" He looked at me, somewhat annoyed that I had interrupted his imaginary foreplay. The girl continued to sit at the edge of his desk, with her legs crossed slightly, twirling her hair teasingly.

"I need a place to stay, I have to move out of Tommy's by tomorrow," I said, this time a bit more desperately.

"Stay here," he raised his hands to the top of the skate shop.

I looked around the skateboard shop. It was in an old building in one of Bakersfield's earliest business districts. The store was long and narrow when you first walked through the door, with slanted racks of shirts and pants on display hanging from the splatter painted walls. The front part of the shop was about twenty feet long to the glass case with a cash register on it. Behind the check out stand was a wall which led to the back portion of the shop, where skateboards were plastered on a black painted wall stretching thirty feet tall.

In the back room, up a steep flight of neon green stairs to the left, where we were now sitting, was a little office, or rather a dusty loft where he had thrown a desk and some old boxes of clothes. The shop had a toilet and a sink, but that was pretty much it; no refrigerator, no shower, no kitchen. I was going to have to live on top ramen noodles made with sink water and a microwave. Could I do it?

"Live here?" I asked, somewhat doubtfully, although still desperate with nowhere else to go.

"Yeah, yeah," he said distantly, his eyes refocused on the giggling blonde girl as he pretended to lick her leg.

I figured that I didn't have a choice, and my often over ambitious optimism got the best of me thinking that living there could help me do even more business. So, with no other choice, I packed up all my stuff once again (for the fifteenth time in two years) and moved into the top of the shop.

And now, things are good, yes, yes, everything is great. I have a place to live and Tyson is letting me use his lifted Chevy truck…A dream come true, ah yes, so many aspiring prayers and hopes and dreams and now, yes now, they are all coming true.

The next morning, before the sun came up, although I wouldn't have known that because there are absolutely no windows in the back of the shop, I get a phone call from Tyson on the shop's phone. It rang loudly, like a drunken monk at a monastery with a huge bell.

RING…RING…RING…RING…!!!

My voice, tired and torn, "Hello?"

"Good morning precious, time to get up…"

It's Tyson. He operates on three hours of sleep. He's a mad man of sorts, and had I not been so focused on my own well being, I would've realized that he was crazy. Yes, he was insane. Bi-polar? Manic?

"What?" I ask.

"I'm coming by the shop, I'm buying another building around the corner, two stores down from the Dugout." He said, and as he says this I realize that it is way too early in the morning to be that enthusiastic.

A few minutes later we are walking down the gray sidewalk next to the side-by-side business district buildings. The downtown stores were more than a hundred years old, the architecture different from one to another.

"This is it," he said, smiling, dangling the keys.

I looked at the front. To the side there are two giant window cases about fifteen feet long caressing two glass doors in the center, which split in the middle. Tyson opened the doors and stepped inside. My eyes widened as they focus towards the back of the empty building, about seventy feet back. My head arches at an angle and looks up at the ceilings, about twenty five feet tall.

"This place is huge," I said, following him to the back.

He grinned.

"What are you going to do with this place?"

He shrugged his shoulders, "I don't know, maybe put a skate ramp, or move the clothing store over here."

As he says this I think of my friend Tyler Durden. Tyler and I were like brothers walking through the same valleys of life; he struggled along the alley of addiction just as much as I did. Durden was a clean cut guy my age with perfectly molded black hair and wore thin wired glasses. By the looks of him, you'd think that he was Denis the Menace's dad and probably sang for the church choir. He liked to sing alright, but it certainly wasn't in church. As soon as you gave the mild mannered looking guy a microphone, he began yelling and screaming and screeching death metal lyrics that would give an old lady a heart attack.

"You should throw concerts here," I suggested to Tyson, thinking in the back of my mind that Tyler and I could gather hundreds, if not thousands of young punks into the building for concerts that would go down in history.

He shrugged his shoulders.

Later that day I brought Durden down to the shop to get his input.

His cheesy greasy grin gave it all away; I knew exactly what he was thinking before I even mentioned the same thought...

"You should tell Tyson to make this into a concert hall...it'd be rad, we could have bands play here, charge five dollars a head and just shut down Jerky's Pizza," Durden said with devilish desire.

As he said this, I realized that he was on to something, however, he was also onto something in the fact that we would have to compete with Jerky's Pizza just three hundred feet around the corner. Jerky's Pizza was a small pizza parlor with a dark and dank basement, where a thirty something year old punk rocker named Nick put on local high school punk bands. This seemed like a challenge, but in reality, it was only a bigger problem…Nick had the punk scene locked down like a monopoly and there was no way in hell he was going to let somebody come in and invade his turf; especially not Tyler who had himself performed many times in the small staged basement.

"What about Nick?" I asked.

"What about him? Why would bands want to play in a dirty basement when they could be playing in a concert hall like this?" He said defiantly, lifting up his arms to show off the huge building.

"Yeah," I said, "You're right."

"Ya think Tyson would be down for something like this?" He asked.

As he asked this, Tyson came cruising through the door with a blonde girly girl curled around his arm.

"Tyson, so perfect for you to come at this very opportune time," I said like a sold out salesman.

"What?" He said, half smirking and giggling while staring at the girl making her giggle too.

"This is my friend Tyler Durden," I said as the two shook hands, although Tyson's hand was still wrapped around the girl's waist.

He grinned.

She giggled.

I smirked, as did Tyler with a sideways glance towards my direction.

"Tyler has some ideas about this place, don't ya Durden?"

Tyler looked at me as if being put on the spot.

"Um, yeah," he said, "You should make this place into a concert hall…charge people five bucks a head to get in, have bands play, make a few hundred dollars a weekend. You could even make it your clothing store during the week."

"Nope," Tyson said without a second's thought. "Too much liability, people will steal stuff. It's going to be a clothing store."

Tyler and I looked at each other with mutual disappointment.

Although Tyson said no, we still had hopes of doing it our way. But I figured Tyson hadn't really thought about it and sure enough when he returned to the store later that night with a different group of people, people all under 25, people who he had just met at the bar next door, Tyson began telling everyone about *his* idea… "Yeah, I'm going to have concerts here, and build a stage and have the best parties ever!"

Tyler and I looked at each other, somewhat sarcastically because Tyson was claiming it to be his idea, but also hopeful, because the ball was now rolling in our direction, regardless of *whose* idea it was.

The next few days and weeks were a whirlwind. What started out as a cool idea, soon became a man made mission to not only build the stage and promote it, but to open the debut on April 20th, better known as the herb smoker's holiday, 420, because long ago it became a stoner ritual to smoke pot at 4:20 everyday, therefore 420 was the biggest stoner day of the year.

For three weeks Tyler and I worked 18 hour days ripping up old orange carpeting, painting the massive walls a deep blood red, and fixed things that need to be fixed while

Tyson would stop in for an hour and shout at us for not working hard enough, or long enough, or good enough.

"I'm so tired," Tyler told me, flushing a paint brush up and down for the millionth time at three in the morning.

Tyson was still buzzing around like a bee shouting, "On it! You gotta be *On It* if you want to get anything done!"

Tyson was always full of energy. "I'm 38 and I'm running circles around you two knuckle heads! Now pick up that paint brush and get that wall finished, I'm going to start welding the stage! Get On It!"

Tyler and I shook our heads. Within those few shorts weeks, we had to find bands, make flyers, paint the building, build the stage, get things organized and above all we had to put up with Tyson the drill sergeant who was as smooth as sandpaper when emotions were already worn thin.

Finally, April 20th had come, and we were exhausted yet excited about the concert debut. Tyler had declared himself the "band manager," so it was his responsibility to make sure all the bands were lined up and ready to go at 7 o'clock. I had made all the flyers and had them passed out to local high schools and other places, so I figured my part of the job was done, although I still had to maintain the skateboard shop around the corner. Tyson was still working frantically on the three foot tall welded wooden stage that was 20 feet by 20 feet. "Come on guys, get On It!" He shouted, "We're not done yet, we still have two hours before the show starts!"

As he said this, dirty Nick from Jerky's Pizza came walking through the door with a smug smirk on his face, "What's up guys, what's going on here?"

Although he asked the question, he already knew the answer; it doesn't take long for word to leak out in a small neighborhood in Bakersfield what was planning to happen.

Tyson stood up with his welding mask over his head, "Oh," he said evasively, "We're just going to have some bands tonight for the opening of our clothing store, no big deal, just a one time thing."

Nick swiped his long natty black hair back. I **stare**d at him quietly looking at his dirty black boots and black shorts and black punk rock shirt. "Cool guys, have fun."

Then he walked out with a devilish laugh.

"God! I hate that guy!" Tyson shouted to himself. "Thinks he owns the place, just walks in here! I'll punch his face off!"

I looked at Tyler's nervous eyes, he knew trouble was brewing.

"He's always up to something," Tyler told Tyson. "He tried to shut another band place down last year. He always plays dirty, you gotta watch out for him."

"I've got the best damn lawyers in town!" Tyson roared. "I'll own that guy if he even thinks of messing with me!"

Tyson threw a wrench to the ground wrathfully as he looked at his watch. "It's 4:30," he said irritated, "The concert is in two and a half hours, when are the bands coming?" He turned asking Tyler.

Tyler hesitated, and dipped the paint brush into the paint to buy some time, then stuttered, "Eh, um, well, only two of the bands are definitely coming for sure…the other three said they'll be here around eight o'clock."

Tyson's wild blue eyes exploded with ecstatic violence, "What the hell? I give you two knuckle heads an opportunity to do something you want to do, but you can't even find five bands in this damned town? Crying out loud, guys, get on it! I've forked out a lot of money for you guys to just be dinking around! Get on it or else we're shutting the whole thing down!" He shouted, his round goateed face turning red and evil.

Tyler and I took a deep breath and held it, waiting for the moment to pass.

Tyson shook his head as he began welding again, when suddenly three fire marshals walked through the door. Tyler and I stood stupid still, as Tyson tried to casually greet the unexpected officers.

"What's going on here?" The head marshal asked, his arms folded across his black buttoned shirt below his golden badge. Tyson flipped from being the fiery drill sergeant, to a nice and charming guy who was out to help the world, something Tyler and I began to call the "Tyson Tango", when his two dueling personalities would switch in a second.

"Oh, hey guys," Tyson said warmly, like old time friends, then he looked around, with the welder's mask over his head, "Um, we're just having some bands play here tonight, no big deal, just have a few friends over to debut the new skate shop," he began, fluffing it up to a 'no big deal' type of thing.

The two officers behind the main marshal stood cross armed as well, with their sunglasses with the little loop strap that wraps around their head, smacking gum with authority as they eyed the building for fire hazard violations.

The main marshal spoke again, eyeing over the place and Tyson's demeanor, "Well, the problem is, we got an anonymous phone call a few minutes ago saying that you were having a concert here and the caller mentioned that this building isn't approved for an event like that."

Tyson's **stare** sizzled with quiet riot anger, he knew who had called, but he kept his cool and kept playing it off as a one-time-no-big-deal-at-all type of thing…just a few people, a few bands, you know, no big deal at all.

One of the assisting officers began walking around calling out fire code violations. "That door in the back needs a push handle for an emergency exit…this room can only hold a hundred people safely…and, this room," he said chomping like a commander on his gum as Tyson was squirming in his skin, "this room needs fire detectors…if you are going to have concerts here and you don't have these things, we can fine you with some heavy fines for all these violations."

Tyler and I **stare**d at Tyson to watch what maneuvers he might use to get himself through this one, and sure enough, he had some more tricks up his sleeve.

"Hey, you guys look familiar," Tyson said, smiling, friendly, unthreatening. The marshals raised an eyebrow, slightly on guard with Tyson's tactics, "Yeah, I've met you guys before, at my brother Frank's house...you know Frank, he's the fire captain for the east side precinct. You guys were there at his New Year's Eve party a few months ago, how have ya guys been?"

And from there, Tyson and the fire marshals began chatting like old buddies, and Tyler and I looked at each other with great relief and slight amazement that Tyson could work out such an odd shot. By the time the officers left, Tyson had them laughing and joking and saying things like, 'Well ya'll have fun tonight...tell your brother we came by to say hi...just fix those things sometime so we don't get any more calls.'

Tyson continued to smile as they walked out the door, then, as they turned the corner out of view and out of earshot, Tyson shouted, "That bastard!" He said of Nasty Nick. Tyler and I looked at the veins popping out of his neck as his face became a furious fire red.

"I'm gonna punch that son of a," Tyson began swearing for the next twenty minutes as we finished up the stage.

By the time we had put the finishing touches, or, as much as we could anyway, on the stage and the building and what not, Tyson told us he was leaving to go get cleaned up at home and not to let Nick or any of his spies in.

We nodded.

Then Tyson sat on his pearl white Harley, strapped his small black helmet to the top of his head, and then peeled out of the building, out the door, and on to the street, leaving a big wide black burnout mark across the plywood floors.

I sat down on the recently finished stage and let my feet dangle from the side. Tyler walked over and collapsed next to me, lying on his back, staring at the ceiling.

"What the hell have we gotten ourselves into, bro?" Tyler asked, on the verge of a nervous break down.

I took a deep breath, paused, replayed the past three weeks in my mind, before I even knew Tyson, or the skate shop or the building, and just shook my head, "I don't know, man. This is going to be crazy. Last month we didn't even know Tyson, and now, he owns us. He's freaking crazy…if tonight doesn't go well, I have no idea what's going to happen."

Tyler lifted his thin wire glasses from his nose and rubbed his eyes, his thin white face and his molded combed hair.

I **stare**d out the front glass windows, to the busy 19th street buzz where people were beginning to walk back and forth to their favorite bars, getting drunk, not caring about any cares in the whole wide world. Yet, with all their careless carousing, I knew and felt, that I had all of their cares and all the cares of the entire world within my soul. With that sensation, I wanted to jump through my skin and shout and scream and tell this world…the only world I have ever known, to leave me the hell I alone, because I was tired and I was frustrated and I…yes I…had had enough.

But, despite my 19-year-old yearnings, I withheld all of the world's worries within my heart and soul and mind. I swallowed my soul as I had done for the past three years since my mom died, and I **stare**d at the ceiling, praying, that God would use this reason or any reason at all, to make it all okay…to make it all worth it.

And yet, with all the emptiness in the open sky above, I couldn't help but feel trapped inside the rat cage of my life. I couldn't help but feel obligated to all the imaginary illusions of my mind. I couldn't help but feel, that my time, the only time I knew to be real...was now...and that time was coming to an end.

Yet, despite those feelings...despite those yearnings, I had to put them aside, and go back to the skate shop around the block, to make myself some Top Ramen noodles with sink water and a microwave... the concert was going to start in an hour.

CHAPTER
THIRTY ONE

"420 Follies…"

Seven o'clock rolled around and the bands were beginning to
show up. I walked outside the front of the concert hall and
saw Bruce at the corner playing his guitar. Bruce was a
bearded longhaired hippie homeless man whom lived off the
money that people threw into his guitar case. I often talked
to him and gave him money when I passed by. The first time
I had come across Bruce was when he was sitting in the
downtown Jack in the Box. He was drinking coffee; loudly
talking to himself, saying that he had drank a cup of LSD

before. He was talking as if he was possessed. Needless to say, I found him interesting.

I walked to the corner and greeted him, "What's up Bruce?"

"H-eeeey m-aaaan…," he spoke as if he recognized my face but was unsure of my name, although I had told him numerous times.

"Hey we are having a concert tonight, and we want you to be our opening act!"

"Far out m-aaaan!" Bruce said with hippie delight.

"Be there in thirty minutes okay?"

"Right on m-aaaan." He said giving me a peace sign.

I walked back feeling somewhat better that I was going to help the guy out. I'm sure he'd feel like a rock star and I thought people would get a kick out of him.

Slowly people began to show up. First a group of five people walked up, then two, then another six. All of them were paying five bucks a head. A big burly friend of Tyson's was manning the door and handling the cash. Tyler and I were still on pins and needles, two bands still hadn't shown up and other little dramas were occurring by the minute.

Some people were bringing in Jack Daniels and other alcohol. It didn't take long before the people were drinking. Not a good idea when most of them were minors and underage. Then Bruce comes walking through the door, and I'm relieved to see him so I can get the show started. "Hey m-aaaan, tell them my stage name is, 'Bruce Berry High Water'," he said slightly slurred.

I got up on the stage and grabbed the microphone in front of the crowd of forty or so high school kids. "Ladies and gentlemen, boys and girls of all ages we are proud to present to you our opening act, Bruce Berry High Water!"

Don't ask me why he insisted on me announcing him this way. He came up on stage and was slightly swerving. *'For crying out loud he's drunk too,'* I thought to myself. This night was snow balling into a disaster right before everyone's eyes.

"Thank you!" He said nearly knocking the microphone over with his acoustic guitar. The people applauded. They were quite receptive to him.

"I'd like to start off with an old favorite of mine..." He said, slowly strumming his guitar.

"Why don't you play with my dingle ling,

oh why don't you

play with my dingle ling..."

He started playing enthusiastically. The crowded started clapping along with him; it was funny watching him and the crowd singing in unison. Everyone was laughing and having a fun time.

Five minutes passed...then ten...then twenty. The once funny Bruce Berry High Water was now the annoying drunk guy on stage. Tyson walked through the door and asked, "What the hell is going on?"

"That's Bruce, our opening act."

"He sounds horrible," Tyson said disgusted.

By this time Bruce was just mumbling and slurring on the microphone somewhat oblivious to the crowd, off in his own little world. People began booing him and yelling at him to get off the stage. Tyson marched up to the front of the platform, "Get the hell off!" He demanded.

"Screw off," Bruce yelled back still playing obnoxiously.

Tyson ripped the microphone away from him and lunged at Bruce grabbing him by the jugular. My heart stopped. I meant the best of intentions for Bruce, I had no idea that he'd come in drunk and make chaos. Bruce cursed at Tyson, "YOU'RE RUDE! YOU'RE RUDE! DON'T EVER TAKE AWAY MY MICROPHONE!"

Tyson and the doorman drug him out to the front and told him to kick rocks. I felt horrible. Tyler got the next band ready up on stage. A group of drunken sixteen year olds started playing erratically in hard-core punk rock fashion. The music was fast and the lyrics were incoherent: everything that punk should be. People began slamming into each other and bouncing off the walls. It was like watching a ritual of an ancient tribe circling around in what is called a pit. They were pounding against each other releasing built up anger and hostility in a somewhat unified punk rock manner.

Other bands went on and the night was becoming more stressful. Teenagers were drunk and causing fights outside the front. There are a lot of police on 19th street because it is in the heart of the downtown bar scene. It didn't take long before Nick was snooping around outside looking for something to sink his teeth into. He tipped off the police saying that there were drunken teens at our place.

Five minutes before the cops showed up I had a gut feeling the night was about to turn to the worst. I was already frustrated with the situation and I just wanted to get away. I told my girlfriend we should leave, and we retreated to the quiet darkness of the skate shop around the corner.

"I had to get out of there," I said nearly at the end of my wit.

We stayed at the store until we heard a pounding on the door. It was Tyson. He looked panicked. I opened the door, "What's going on?"

"The cops just busted it. There were some kids in the front drinking and they busted them. I ducked out the back," He said wide-eyed. It was uninspiring to see that Tyson was so quick to jump ship and not defend it like a fearless captain should. Instead, Tyler got the blame.

Unfortunately for Tyler, the cops busted him for some old parking tickets and hauled him off to jail. The cops shut the concert hall down and confronted Tyson about underage drinking but didn't do anything else. We spent the rest of the night getting Tyler out of jail.

The next morning I woke up defeated. Maybe it was all just a bad dream I thought optimistically. Unfortunately it wasn't. I was looking for a way out of the situation but I was trapped. I kept getting thoughts of moving down south with my Aunt Beth and Uncle Craig, my Dad's brother and sister. They lived on a 34-acre ranch down in the Ortega Mountains.

'If I just got up and moved 250 miles away from all this drama and just deserted everyone and everything, would I be wrong for that?' I thought to myself. I just put it off, thinking that it was an unrealistic escape, but I often day dreamed what it would be like to leave it all behind.

Three more weeks went by of the same turmoil at the concert hall and clothing store. Everyday drama lurked around the corner. The other employee at the skate shop, Danielle, was getting tired of Tyson treating her rudely and not paying her on time. The concert hall was always a disaster and was bringing Tyler and I a bad name. We were struggling to keep the sinking ship afloat, but the weight of controversy was crushing it quickly.

After a hectic weekend in early May, I found myself frustrated and completely broken. I took out a sheet of paper and wrote a letter. That letter of desperation would end up changing my life forever...

CHAPTER
THIRTY TWO

"A Letter Forever Changed..."

Sitting at my desk above the skate shop which was my dreaded room of entrapment, I wrote a letter to God. I told God that I was tired and frustrated and that I wanted out of this hole I had dug for myself. I wrote a tear-stained letter of desperation, pleading with God to change my life.

I had been keeping a journal of the activities that were happening in my life on my computer. I read through it and recognized a gradual decline. I saw that the opportunity that I had once thought was a blessing, turned out to be a lesson learned: Be careful what you ask for because you might just get it.

This time however, I was asking God to make something happen. I didn't know what it was going to be, but I just wanted him to make his move. I knew that he was perfectly capable of it but I figured I just had to ask Him to do it.

After I signed the letter to God, I read over it hoping that it could be true. Then the phone rang. I answered it and it was my dad down in Corona Del Mar. My dad's voice came through in a concerned tone, "Is something wrong? I just got this feeling to call you, are you okay?" My dad was a pretty intuitive guy and recognized gut feelings when he got them.

"No dad, I can't take it anymore. I just want to give up. There is too much drama," I said nearly choked up with tears.

I explained to him what was going on and that I couldn't handle the pressure anymore. I told him that I had been keeping a journal of the events, and I read him some of the things that I had written. He told me it made an interesting story. He said it could make a good book someday. I just laughed at first, but then it struck me, *'Perhaps this is why I had gone down these paths in life: to write a book!'*

It was like an epiphany. *'Oh I get it now!'* I thought eagerly. The pressure disappeared. *'Wow, maybe all this should be a book!'* I thanked my dad for his inspiration. I thought I had gotten my answer.

The joy of my revelation was soon deflated as the second phone line rang through. "I have to go dad, bye," I said switching to the second line.

It was Tyson. "What's going on?" He asked on his static filled cell phone.

"Danielle and Tyler want their checks, they have to pay rent today and need their money," I said on behalf of my employees.

"Well that's too bad, I'm headed to the golf course," he said completely unconcerned for the welfare of my employees. I was infuriated.

"What do you mean that's too bad! They need their money, Tyson, or else Danielle is going to be evicted from her apartment. When are you going to bring the checks?" I questioned defensively.

"I'll be there when I'm done. If they don't like it, tell them to kick rocks!" Click. He hung up on me. I lost it.

"That's it, I'm over it!" I shouted as I slammed the phone down.

I began boxing up all my stuff in the skate shop. I took Tyson's big truck and packed all my stuff in the back. I drove over to Tyler's mom's house where he was staying and told him that I quit and that I needed to stay with him for a few days. He looked at me and realized that I was serious. I moved my stuff into his garage, and then we went and floated in his pool. It was our first break in nearly thirty days. In my mind I had completely written off the shop. I had shut the store down and I knew that Tyson would be furious, but because of his uncaring attitude, I didn't care.

"So what are you going to do now?" Tyler asked as we were floating on rafts amidst the calmness of his pool.

"I'm going to write a book," I said.

"Haha, are you serious?" He asked laughing, unsure if I was being sarcastic.

"Yep, I'm serious. I think I'm going to move down to my Aunt Beth's. They have a ranch up in the mountains. It'll be a total retreat and I can write my book over the summer," I said optimistically and somewhat naively thinking that I could write the book in such a short amount of time.

"How are you going to get all your stuff down to Ortega?" He asked, looking up at me with his hand blocking the sun from his eyes.

I just smiled at him and asked sarcastically, "Oh by the way Tyler, will you drive me down to Ortega?" He laughed as he realized that I wasn't really asking him; I was implying to him that he was already recruited for the job. He flipped over my raft playfully. "Yeah I'll take you. When do you want to leave?"

"How about Sunday?" I said.

"Mother's day?" He said somewhat unsure if that was a good day to leave.

"Yeah…Mother's day, that's a good day to make the trip," I thought with remembrance of my mother.

"Alright Mr. Author, I'll take you Sunday."

CHAPTER
THIRTY THREE

"Ortega Odyssey…"

She would often make brownies in the kitchen. When I was at school, she would clean the house. When I was sick, she would make me chicken noodle soup. If I were bad, she would discipline me. If I were good, she would reward me. All the things that mom's do and yet you never truly appreciate them until they are gone forever.

I no longer have the chance to give my mom a hug, and kiss her on the cheek telling her Happy Mother's day. I can't take her out to breakfast and show her my appreciation for all the wonderful things that she had done for me in my life. Instead, I'm on my way to my aunt's house 250 miles away in the Ortega Mountains, determined to write a book about my life.

I sat in the passenger seat of Tyler's mom's car listening to the radio. I was staring off into the upcoming mountains, still trying to figure out if I really knew what I was doing. *'Writing a book? What am I crazy?'* I thought to myself. Perhaps it was just my excuse to leave Bakersfield and all the horrible things that had happened in the past month and the past two years for that matter.

We made our way to the twisty two-lane road of Ortega highway. It was notorious for accidents, due to vertical cliffs and twisty turns. It took us about forty-five minutes to get up the windy mountain.

We arrived at a little village that had a beef jerky store and some small houses around it. It was a small community of about twenty people. I saw my Aunt's mailbox off to the side of the road and told him to turn in after it. We drove down a dirt path for about five hundred feet. The road sloped down steeply as it came underneath a canopy of huge oak trees, some reaching seventy feet tall.

The treetops provided a peaceful shade over the little house where my aunt lived. Off to the right was an old barn where Uncle Craig made cabinets for his wood working business. He was a big burly manly man that made stuff with his hands. Tyler's car made a ruckus as we drove over the pebbled rocks near the front gate. A swarm of dogs came running out of the house barking.

"Is this a farm?" Tyler asked somewhat sarcastically.

"Sort of, it's more like a ranch than a farm." I answered.

We stepped out of the car relieved to be at our destination. The dogs stopped barking at us and went about chasing each other around.

"What's up JB?" Beth called out from inside the house with a thick Georgian accent. She had lived in Georgia for several years, and I hadn't really been as close to her as I was with my other aunts.

"What's up Beth?" I responded walking towards the house. Tyler followed me, asking me where the bathroom was. "Just go over there." I said sarcastically pointing towards a tree. "No seriously dude, I've gotta go." He said doing the pee pee dance.

We went inside the house and my aunt gave me a big hug. "Where's the bathroom?" Tyler asked nearly wetting himself. Beth showed him the restroom and he raced off.

"Ya'll have a good trip I take it?" She asked with southern style.

"Yeah, not bad. I'm glad to be here."

"I still have to drive back up." Tyler said in dread, as he contemplated making the drive again.

"Kick yer feet up and sit a while." Beth encouraged as she made us something to eat.

I went outside and checked out my new surroundings. It was a completely different pace of life up there. The house was small and smelled like dogs. The trees and plant life flourished around the ranch making the atmosphere feel charmed. Birds were singing in the background, and the dogs continued to growl and wrestle with each other.

I walked up a windy dirt path, which passed by a cactus garden that was blossoming pink flowers. Trees were everywhere and their shedding leaves littered the ground. I followed the dirt path up to the horse barn. Next to it was Beth's black stallion named Tony; a beautiful black horse with lean cut muscle. Beth was a typical cowgirl; Cowboy boots, jeans and a t-shirt crowned by her trademark brown cowboy hat. She was full of life and full of stories.

Walking nearly three hundred feet from the house, I came up to a broken down tractor that was above the horse coral. I sat atop the broken down tractor and took in the panoramic view. From up there, I could see the surrounding mountaintops of Ortega. I could also see the tree canopy that covered the house below. I took in a deep breath and thought back a week.

Just a week before, I was stuck in a horrible situation in Bakersfield at Wicked Hall. I remember writing the letter to God pleading for him to make things different. I marveled at how quickly he made it change, literally within minutes of writing the letter. I was living an answered prayer and I wanted to make the best of it. I sat there for a moment and let it all set in.

I ventured back down to the house and began to unload my belongings from Tyler's cram packed car.

"Put all your fixings in here." Beth said in her southern drawl while showing me which room I was going to stay in. I organized the boxes and put the last of my stuff in the spare room.

"Are you sure you want to do this?" Tyler asked once more, giving me a final chance to change my mind and go back up to Bakersfield with him.

"Yes, I'm sure. I have to. It's meant to be."

"Everything happens for a reason, right?" He said with a smile referring to my often quoted belief.

"That's right. Everything happens for a reason." I said smiling.

We gave each other a big handshake and he drove back up the dirt path in which we had come. I watched him as he drove off, repeating to myself what he had said, "Everything happens for a reason…everything happens for a reason."

Later on that night, I settled down on the couch and watched the Sopranos with Beth. I was relaxed and feeling happy that everything turned out for the best. Suddenly the dogs began to bark, as we heard a car drive across the noisy rocks near the gate entrance. I was startled wondering who it could possibly be.

"Are you expecting anybody?" I asked Beth.

"Naw, that's just Baby Jack." Beth said.

"Who?"

"Jackson, he's the black carpenter that works with Craig. They've been friends for years and he's staying up here during the week to work with Craig." She answered, still watching television.

The door opened and the dogs came running in, the smallest dog leaping up and barking at Jackson as he came in holding his luggage.

"You look here, you stop barking at me, you hear, it's just me Jackson; you know what I'm saying huh?" He told the dog as if it could understand him. The dog tilted his head sideways in confused way, then ran off.

"Hey Beth, how ya'll doing? I had a good time down in San Bernardino; you know what I'm saying, huh?" Jackson said to Beth. "But I ran out of money Beth; you know what I'm saying, huh? Craig needs to get back and pay me more; you know what I'm saying, huh? I need money to live Beth." He said slightly whining. Beth kept her eyes on the television, "I know what your saying Baby Jack." Why she called him Baby Jack, I have no idea.

I found it interesting that after everything he said, he would follow up with 'you know what I'm saying, huh?' I fixated on this repetitive saying in my mind. I found it humorous.

"Hi, I'm Saulanis Jackson," He said sticking out his hand.

"I'm Craig's nephew, John." I responded back.

"Is Craig going to pay you to work with us? Because I need more money; you know what I'm saying, huh?" He carried on with his financial woes and his now trademark saying.

"I know what you're saying." I said going along with the theme.

After the arrival of Jackson had settled, we all three sat and watched the Sopranos. During a commercial break Beth and I got into a conversation about destiny and life paths. I told her about how I thought God had me on a journey and how everything was unfolding perfectly in a somewhat coincidental way. Everything just seemed to click, and my quest for reason left me determined.

"I've got an awesome book for you to read." She said as she darted in her room to get the book.

"THE LIFE YOU WERE BORN TO LIVE," she read the cover.

"What's it about?" I asked eagerly.

"When you are born you have a birth number that relates to your patterns and paths that you will take in life," she began to explain in her Georgian accent.

"What's mine?" I asked enthusiastically.

"When's your birthday?"

"August 12, 1981."

"Alright that would be an 8 for August, plus 1 plus 2, plus 1, plus 9, plus 8, plus 1 which equals 30. You take the 3+0, which would equal a 30/3. Then you take that number and look up the reference of your life challenges," she said thumbing through the pages to my related section.

"Interesting," she said reading it over to herself.

"What? What does it say? Is it good?" I asked anxiously.

"It says that you are on a life path to work through issues of expression and sensitivity, overcoming self doubt to express yourself and to use your inner gifts to encourage, uplift, and inspire others," she read. "The greatest gift of 30/3s lies in *expression* and *inspired communication*. Whether through speaking, acting, *writing*, or art, they find joy in moving others emotionally, perhaps moving them to action, to change, or to happiness. In the positive, their effectiveness comes from an ability to speak and write with feeling -- not just from the mind, but from the heart."

My eyes lifted in excitement feeling that those words summed me up perfectly. She handed me the book and I read every page related to my path. My focus went from my troubles to now discovering my life's purpose. I was eager to obtain as much knowledge as I could from her books. I read through everything she had and was beginning to feel enlightened.

For the first couple of days at the ranch, I would just relax underneath an oak tree swaying back and forth in a hammock reading books pertaining to destiny. My eyes were being opened to the fact that all my "life coincidences" were in fact no coincidences at all. They were merely proverbial forks in the path of life. I was on a journey of self-discovery and was becoming increasingly intuitive. I began reflecting over my life and reviewed all of the coincidences, trying to map my path's pattern.

I began writing my book with all this new found intuition. The first thing I wrote was the chapter in this book, *EVERYTHING HAPPENS FOR A REASON.* I wasn't sure if it was good or not until my family came up to visit us at the ranch.

My aunts and uncles all gathered at the ranch. Somewhere along the line, it came up that I was writing a book.

"What's your book about?" My aunt Mary who was visiting from Boston asked.

"I'm not really sure yet. I've only written a chapter so far." I said.

"Can I read it?" She asked optimistically.

"Sure, why not." I said, feeling somewhat unsure of my writing abilities.

I went in my room and printed out the chapter from my computer. I went back to the living room and handed it to her, "Here you go."

I sat across from her and watched her read it. I was chewing on my thumbnail nervous about revealing my inner most feelings to her on paper. 'Who was I fooling? I'm not a writer,' I thought doubtfully. 'No one could possibly care about my story' I continued thinking negatively until I saw her take off her glasses and wipe tears from her eyes.

"It's beautiful," she said obviously touched by what I had written.

"You like it?" I asked somewhat shocked.

"You're a great writer," she said.

'A writer, wow, that sounded neat, I never really considered myself to be a writer,' I thought to myself.

She passed my writing to my other aunt Barbie who then read the story out loud to the living room full of relatives. By the time she finished, everyone was wiping away tears. I didn't have any idea how powerful writing could be until I experienced that moment.

Writing soon became my purpose. I wrote about everything that was on my mind. I wrote about my hurt and my anger. I typed tenaciously about my depression and addiction. I punched every key with purpose and determination. 'Who am I' was the only thought I focused on.

By mid summer I had a binder full of written memories, thoughts, psychological summaries and a slew of short stories. It was as if I had gone into the bottomless pit of my soul and began mining out all the coals of my life. I took the lumps of coal from my soul, and polished them into diamonds of description and reason.

That summer was a turning point in my life. I was going to be twenty years old in August, and it occurred to me that I wasn't going to be a teenager anymore. I was evolving into a man and I realized that I had to let go of the Peter Pan fantasy of, "I never want to grow up."

When I wasn't discovering my chaotic cavern, I was helping Craig and Jack make cabinets in the old barn. Craig was an aggressive guy who had a short temper. He would often curse and grumble when working. At first it was uncomfortable for me, but then I realized that he wasn't mad at me, he was just mad at the world. I learned to stay out of his way.

"Angry," he'd growl as he looked around the shop for his hammer.

"Jack, do you have my freaking hammer?" Craig barked.

"I didn't take your hammer, Craig. You always leave it on the ground, Craig. You know what I'm saying, huh?" Jack defended himself, still using his cliché.

As angry as Craig was, you couldn't help but marvel at his craftsmanship. He made huge entertainment cabinets and detailed drawers. When we were finished with the masterpieces, we would go down to Irvine and install them into homes usually belonging to a doctor or a lawyer.

"Ten grand," Craig said enthusiastically as he got into the truck after installing a cabinet for a dentist. Craig was paid well for his trade, and he was quite the hustler when it came to getting business. I couldn't help but appreciate the attitude of 'Bringing home the bacon' that he possessed. He really taught me a lot about myself and about following through on your word.

It was nearly August and things at the ranch were peaceful. I spent my days working with Craig or typing at my computer. My aunt Beth and I talked a lot about life and our interpretation of its meaning. Her and I really bonded that summer, which in general made me appreciate my family more. Every time I looked at Craig or Beth I saw my own blood. I felt a sense of tradition. My great grandfather, John Butler the first, was a carpenter. The ability to do wood work was always in the family, which unfortunately stopped with me. I just didn't have the finesse and patience it takes to create a pile of wood into an amazing display case.

In August Craig decided to go into business with another guy named Dave Martin who owned Martin Construction in Anaheim. Craig would drag me out of bed at six in the morning and we'd go down to Martin's wood shop.

Craig was the foreman, and the agreement between Craig and Dave was that Craig could use his woodshop and crew of men, in return for running Dave's various projects. Craig loved bossing people around. He was a lion so it was in his nature. The problem being was that Dave was a lion as well. The clashing of heads didn't take long.

In between their heated discussions of cabinet projects and use of labor, I would work in the office and organize papers for Mr. Martin. He was an organization freak, who had to have everything three hole punched and filed chronologically into a three ring binder. I sifted through stacks of papers and did as he ordered. At the time I thought he was having me do work of importance, but it wasn't until later when I discovered that he was just giving me "busy work" to keep me out of the way. Regardless of his reasons, his insisting of organization taught me another valuable lesson. From then on, I became very efficient in my organization skills.

Dave Martin worked out a deal that if I worked with him and Craig for the month of August, then he would give me $1,000. I was willing to do whatever busy work he wanted of me, because my goals were now focused on returning to Bakersfield and getting an apartment by the end of the month so I could start school for the fall quarter.

I toughed it out and put up with the two lions. They both taught me a lot about business and what it takes to be a leader. I observed their tactics and saw how they used determination to get deals they wanted.

I spent the last few days at the ranch trying to organize my return to Bakersfield. My girlfriend gave me phone numbers from the newspaper of available rooms for rent. I called the number she gave me and got a hold of an old man name Armand. I could tell that he had some type of accent, which sounded Cuban, and I was somewhat unsure of moving in with him because I had never moved in with a complete stranger before. I told him that I was coming up to Bakersfield on Saturday August 23rd. I told him that I

173

needed to move in the same day so I could start school on the 25th. He told me to check out the house and we would discuss it then.

On the day before I was going to leave for Bakersfield, Dave paid me my $1,000 and I had arranged for some Dickweed shirts to be printed for that same day. I sold some of the shirts quickly to the cabinetmakers in the shop. Dave agreed to let me borrow his white Ford pick up truck to make my move, but I had to return the vehicle the same day, which would entail making my move, returning the vehicle, and then riding the bus back to Bakersfield all within a twelve hour period.

I packed up my stuff in the truck on the last night. I walked up to the tractor and sat there, staring at the stars reflecting over my summer at the ranch. I prayed out loud, "God, I know you had this all planned and I thank you. Please help me make this move. Father please help me make this transition to Bakersfield. I don't know where I'll stay or where I'll work, but I know you will provide. Thy will be done." A shooting star streaked across the heavens. I knew my prayer was received. I just had to go to sleep and wait for the morning to continue on my journey.

CHAPTER
THIRTY FOUR

"The Return to Bakersfield…"

I woke up Saturday morning before the sun came up and took my last shower at the ranch. After I got dressed, I walked around the house one last time to make sure I hadn't left anything behind. My stuff was already packed in the back of the white Ford. I quietly pulled out from under the massive tree coverage and up the driveway. I looked back in my rear view mirror one last time and took a deep breath. I knew that I was closing one more chapter in my life, and beginning a whole new one. I had mixed feelings of anxiety, uncertainty, and excitement.

I was taking another proverbial jump into the water and learning how to swim. I only had $400 in my pocket and a box of Dickweed shirts. I wasn't even sure if the guy I talked to on the phone would let me rent the room from him. I was just going on the notion that everything would work out perfectly as it should.

As I pulled out onto Ortega Highway to make my long journey back home to Bakersfield, I popped in Eric Clapton's Tears in Heaven into the tape player. As the guitar slowly played, my eyes began to well up with tears. I reflected on my stay at Ortega with my Aunt Beth and Uncle Craig with great joy. I thought about all the things that brought me there in first place. I even thought about Jackson and his infamous conversations about himself. I couldn't help but realize that my stay at Ortega was a major turning point in my life; both spiritually and psychologically.

After I made it down the hill, I made a quick stop at Jack in the Box. I sat in the parking lot and ate a Breakfast Jack as I contemplated what I was about to do. I **stare**d off into the distance in deep analytical thought. I thought about how I was going to make the transfer to Bakersfield and start a whole new life. My marketing class would be starting in less than forty-eight hours. Within those forty-eight hours I had to; find a place to live, buy my book for class, move my stuff in, drive back down to Anaheim to return the truck, and catch a train/bus back to Bakersfield. I sped out of the parking lot completely determined and focused.

I pulled into my girlfriend's house just a little before noon. She was ecstatic to see me and I was happy to be back in her arms. I had put her through a lot during our relationship, and moving 250 miles away was the biggest challenge she had to face. It wasn't fair to her, but it was something that I had to do that summer. Either way, we were both happy it all worked out.

I called up the guy I had spoken with the other night about coming by and seeing if he'd rent me a room. My girlfriend and I drove up there and met him. He was a retired sixty-two year old Cuban teacher. We sat down with him and told him how important it was that I move in that day. Luckily he agreed and I moved my stuff into my new room. I paid him for the first month's rent and then my girlfriend and I headed off to Bakersfield College to get my book for my marketing class that was starting in two days. I was shocked to see that I had paid $45 for the class but had to pay $115 for the book. That completely took all of my money, but I had no other choice.

Next on the list was to return the truck back down to Martin Construction in Anaheim so we could catch a train by five o'clock. I was tired so I let my girlfriend drive. It was her first time encountering LA traffic but she got us to the train station by 4:45. Martin Construction was about two miles away, and we had initially planned to leave the truck at the shop, and walk back to the train station. However if we did that, there was no way that we would have made the train. I had to call my uncle Craig and tell him that he'd have to pick up the truck at the train station, which he wasn't too happy about.

As we boarded the train and made our way back home, I felt relieved that it had all turned out perfectly. Just twelve hours earlier, I was sitting in the Jack in the box parking lot wondering if it was all going to work, and indeed it had. My girlfriend rested her head on my shoulder and we both slept peacefully on the way back up to Bakersfield.

The summer I spent in Ortega was a major transition from being a teenager to becoming a man. When I went down there, I was a troubled nineteen year old looking to escape all that my life had become. That summer was a time of spiritual growth and understanding. I came to realize that all the choices I had made the past three years had led me down the dead end roads of drugs and denial. But now, with

a heart full of hope and a determination to do the right thing,
I came to Bakersfield to start over.

CHAPTER
THIRTY FIVE

"Jake's Tex Mex..."

Now that I had returned to Bakersfield with a new sense of spiritual purpose, I called up Bob. It had been a year since I left his house on a bad note, but he was a gracious and forgiving man, and he told me he was excited to see me again. I know I felt the same. Soon, we began a weekly ritual of meeting at his favorite eating establishment to discuss the things of life, death and, his favorite, of God.

"Meet you at Jake's Tex Mex?"

"You got it," I said smiling.

I popped my head in the door and looked down the long line of people in search of my guest. 'He's not here yet' I thought to myself as I stood behind the last person in line. The chaotically decorated lobby of Jake's Tex Mex entertained my short attention span as I stood there waiting.

With a smile bright and wide, Bob came through the door and stuck out his hand.

"Hey Bob!" I said with a huge grin.

"Hey John!" He responded just as enthusiastically.

"Have you been here long?" He asked.

"Nope, just a few minutes."

The slow rhythmic shuffle of the people's feet in front of us began to pick up. Bob and I looked at the menu on the wall before quickly being asked for our order from a young blonde girl behind the L-shaped counter.

"Half chicken sandwich and cowboy potatoes, please." Bob said with polite exuberance.

"Half a chicken sandwich, please." I told the girl with similar respect as she turned to me.

We grabbed our food trays like freshmen in high school and paid for our meal at the register. "Are there any tables open?" Bob asked.

I looked around and saw that the entire front diner was full. "Nope, I guess it's our usual spot today." I answered back.

With one hand holding a large drink and the other balancing a tray containing our Bibles and sandwiches, we headed to the outside patio area to our typical Thursday table. Unusually enough, no matter how crowded Jake's Tex Mex would be during lunch rush, our table in the corner always seemed to be vacant.

As we situated ourselves at the table, I took off my hat and placed my tray on the chair next to me. I looked up at Bob and with a smile he said, "Let's pray."

With bowed heads and closed eyes Bob began to pray in a humble tone, "Heavenly father, we come before you and thank you for this time we have together. Father we thank you for this meal, and for arranging our schedules so we can spend time together in fellowship. I ask you to bless our time together, and to bless this meal that we are about to receive. In Jesus name, Amen."

Bob's eyes opened slowly and he smiled with joy. We opened up our Bibles and turned to our lesson in our Christian study guide. In between bites of our food, we would quiz ourselves with different memory verses.

"Philippians 4:13," he said in a testing manner.

My eyes **stare**d off to the right thinking of the answer, and then back into Bob's patient blue eyes, "I can do all things through Christ who strengthens me," I said triumphantly. He smiled at my enthusiasm.

"2 Timothy 2:15" I blurted out in a friendly attempt to put his memory to the test.

He took a sip of his ice tea, and then focused his eyes slightly drawing a blank **stare**. He began to chuckle, "start it off" he asked for assistance.

"Be diligent…" I said trying to spark his memory carefully without giving him too much information.

"Oh yeah, 'Be diligent to present yourself approved to God as a workman who does not need to be ashamed, handling accurately the word of truth." He nailed it perfectly, leaving me to somewhat believe that he knew the verse the entire time and that his little stall was just his playful way of letting me think that I had stumped him. I just laughed, feeling somewhat one-upped.

We finished our sandwiches and set our trays and trash onto the table next to us; an employee came by and swooped it up. We continued to quiz one another on our verses and finally stopped when we had reviewed all of them, both of us remembering each one perfectly.

"So how has Christ changed your life, John?" He asked getting more serious.

I looked at his peaceful face and smiled as I tried to compress so many thoughts into a shortened answer. "Gee, that's hard to say." I started off. Bob must have known that it was going to be one of my trademark ramblings as he relaxed himself into his usual spot, leaning against the wall with his feet propped on the bench.

"I look back over my life, from just a year ago and everything has changed. Last September I didn't have a job or a car, and I was renting a room from a 64 year old retired Cuban teacher." I said with a smirk. "Now I have a great job, a van and I have my own apartment."

Bob continued to look at me patiently as if encouraging me to go deeper. "What else?" He urged.

I looked out the window in search of an answer. "Really, I guess I just feel at peace." His eyes lifted as if I were getting closer.

"Before I had Christ I had an emptiness that I tried to fill with drugs. I think that emptiness of course all started when my Mom passed away. Now I am able to read and study the Bible, which is the word of God, and now I am full of hope, peace and joy. I realize now that Christ gave his life for our sins and that I have been forgiven, thus, I no longer have to carry around the guilt of sin. It has been an uplifting experience for sure." I said a bit more confidently.

Bob continued to smile as his right hand reached for his reading glasses in his shirt pocket. "Turn to Ephesians 2:8," he prompted. I grabbed my Bible and turned to the verse.

"For by grace you have been saved through faith; and that not of yourselves, it is the gift of God; not as a result of works, that no one should boast. For we are His workmanship, created in Christ Jesus for good works, which God prepared beforehand, that we should walk in them."

Bob read with the authority of truth as I sat and awaited his follow up explanation. After he finished reading he slid his glasses to the top of his dark charcoal gray hair.

"God has a plan for your life John. But before God could work in your life and get you on track for your plan, you had to receive his gift of eternal life," Bob said with hopeful assurance. "However, sin separates us from God. For God to be able to be with us, we have to accept his son Jesus Christ and ask for forgiveness of our sins. He was sinless and therefore He is the only one worthy before God. When we accept Christ, we ourselves become sinless. It's as if Jesus is the filter and God sees us through Jesus," Bob's wise explanation rang true in my ears.

"If I got John Butler a present and put it here on the table, but you didn't receive it and accept it, then have I really given you a present?" Bob began to explain, "God gave the world his only begotten son. But it is up to us to receive His son and accept Him. We accept Him by faith alone. We must have faith that He died for our sins to bring us closer to God." Bob finished and **stare**d at me patiently as I mentally digested what he had just said.

"So we aren't saved unless we actually *receive* Christ?" I said.

"Right." He smiled.

"I get it. God has given us this gift, but we have to choose to accept it." I said brightly.

"God wants us to be in Heaven because of his grace. He doesn't want you to earn your way to Heaven on your own merit; it's impossible, because all men have fallen short to the glory of God. You can't earn the kingdom of Heaven, it is a gift." Bob carried on, "He wants us to be submissive to His will and He wants us to accept the gift He has given us so He can work in our lives and use us to help other people."

"So how can I help people?" I asked.

"You can lead them to the Lord." Bob said simply.

"I know. But I find it hard sometimes. There are so many times that I just want to witness to someone but I feel like I'm out of place or that I'm going to say the wrong thing."

Bob smiled at my simplicity. "There is a place and time for everything, John. Perhaps, what you can tell someone is that you've gone through a similar situation, and tell him or her how the Lord helped you. As a witness, you are testifying to other people what Christ has done in your life. They can either choose to accept Him or not. But by giving them a glimpse of what Christ has done in your life, you have planted seeds of hope in their hearts that will some day blossom into a relationship with the Lord."

I looked at Bob with respect. Bob always had a way of explaining things and making them seem so easy. I looked at my watch and realized that it was already two o'clock.

"So I'll see you next Thursday?" I said suggestively.

"Next Thursday." Bob smiled.

We walked outside to the parking lot. I got to my van and set my Bible on the driver seat. I turned around to see Bob with open arms and we gave each other a big bear hug. We parted with a firm handshake and a friendly smile. "God bless," he said.

I looked back at him appreciatively, "Thanks, Bob. God bless."

CHAPTER
THIRTY SIX

IN LOVING MEMORY OF OUR SON, BROTHER
AND NOLAN'S DAD
"THE HIGHLIGHTER"
ADAM SAMUEL PIERCE

DECEMBER 3, 1975   JUNE 22, 2002

METAL ACOUSTA

"Goodbye Adam…"

"Sup Butler?" Adam Pierce asked with his typical confident mischievous grin beneath his helmet.

"Sup Pierce?" I responded in a similar manner, taking off my goggles.

"How long have you been out here riding?" He asked as he leaned his dusty dirt bike next to a cement block in the middle of a field.

"About ten minutes," I said.

"Follow me, I want to show you this new jump," he said, kick starting his bike.

Eager to see what ridiculous suicidal jump he would attempt next, I started my 125 and followed him. The dust coming off his back tire looked like thousands of mini tornados streaming across a desolate terrain. Traveling at the speed that most motorists drive on the freeway, we scurried across the field to a new land of cut out sumps and vertical cliffs. Mounds of dirt dominated the flat terrain, teasing Adam's eagerness and curiosity. *'How big he could go,'* was the only thought that occupied his every waking moment.

His bike roared forward as I trailed behind him about twenty feet; a perfect viewpoint to witness any outrageous leap that he may challenge. Clicking up another gear, he stood up in the attack position directly in front of a twenty-foot vertical cliff. The lump of anxiety in my throat dropped to my stomach as his bike launched towards the heavens with ultimate force.

His body and bike floated in mid air, which seemed like an eternity, completely defying the laws of gravity. At a pinnacle of nearly fifty feet in the air, he threw his body off the back of his airborne machine and with his left hand grabbed the rear of his bike twisting his hips all in one simultaneous fluid motion. As if this weren't testimony enough to insanity and showmanship, in the midst of his lunatic leap, he **stare**d back at me as if to say, "Try this."

As gravity finally caught up with Adam's defiance, he shifted his body back to his re-entry position and boldly threw both wheels of his machine onto the innocent ground beneath. I finally caught my breath again, as Adam parked next to me.

"Did you see that?" He asked.

I paused for a moment; still stunned by what I had just seen. "You're nuts," I said.

"That was an Indian air superman seat grab," he said proudly.

"I learned it at Deegan's," he said referring to his longtime friend and leader of the Metal Mulisha Brian Deegan. Adam had been a professional freestyle motocross rider since the beginning of the sport in 1997. I hadn't ridden with Pierce in a longtime, and his genre of tricks had steadily increased since the last time I had been riding with him...

But now flash forward two years later as I am lost in this fond memory while my girlfriend's voice echoes in and says, "We're here babe."

I broke my daze of reflection and looked out the window to see the entry of the emergency room at Kern Medical Center.

Uncertainty and fear filled my body.

Holding my girlfriend's hand, we walked up to the receptionist desk and asked what room Adam Pierce was in. The overly busy nurse just ignored our request as she dealt with five other concerned people looking for their loved ones.

Knowing that the chaos of her duties would waste valuable time, I cunningly looked on her sheet and saw Adam's name and room number. With slyness, Sarah and I crept through the other lobby. Thinking that we had outwitted the system, our hopes were crushed as we came to a secured door requiring a secret pin number. My eyes clinched in frustration as my soul shouted to God for assistance.

As I reopened my eyes, a male nurse came walking through the door. Wanting to seize the opportunity of God's help, I squeezed my girlfriend's hand and she spoke up, "Where's Adam Pierce's room?"

He stopped and looked at us hesitantly. "Are you guys family? Because only family can be back here to see him." He said, unknowingly fueling my next response.

"Um, yeah. I'm a brother," I said feeling somewhat honest. Adam and I had grown up together since junior high school and I felt as close to him as a brother.

The nurse took us back to where Adam was. My heart stopped as I saw him.

His body lay there lifeless. Machines and tubes synchronized his breathing. Ice packs covered his swollen and purple head. His once determined eyes were now sealed and slightly bleeding. I dropped Sarah's hand as she turned away, obviously disturbed by what she saw. I walked up to Adam and grabbed his hand.

My knees felt weak and my stomach knotted as I **stare**d at him. I stood there for a second, then I felt as though I needed to sit down. I kept reflecting over his life as I sat there. I thought about all the things that he had stood for in his lifetime. I thought about his highs and his lows. Everything he had gone through and survived, and it all came to an end like this.

I remembered his fiery blue eyes and how they revealed of the depths of ambition and confidence. I felt that if I listened closely I could still hear his voice and how it carried an edgy boldness that only he could verbalize. His passion and energy infiltrated a crowded room as quickly as light floods the darkness. One interaction with Pierce was energizing enough to leave you with the feeling that you, too, could take over the world with the same passion that he possessed.

The night before Adam made the mistake of getting into a truck with a drunk driver whom he had just met a few hours before. Apparently, the intoxicated driver was swerving around showing off for Adam. In the blink of an eye, the truck flipped over several times before coming to a rest on Adam's body.

All the times that Adam had cheated death and now death had finally taken its inevitable power position. Adam's time on earth was coming to an end. I sat there astonished. I was lost. I felt the fragility of life. I was once again experiencing death's numbing and humbling ability. My own mortality trembled with fear.

I was only there for a few minutes before Adam's dad and stepmother came rushing in. Ron, Adam's dad, rushed to his son's side and knelt down, completely crushed with a father's broken heart. Tears rolled down his face, as they did mine. The love that Ron had for his son shook me to the core of my being. I sat there speechless.

The nurse came up to Sarah and me and told us that we had to leave. I stood up and tried to say something to Ron, but my voice stopped short, realizing that my words would just fall on deaf ears. As I walked out the room, I said a prayer in my heart for Adam and his family. I felt helpless, but I had to realize that Adam was in God's hands now.

Halfway out the door I looked back, realizing that it would probably be the last time I'd see Adam. I saw Ron praying as well. With tears in my eyes and a lump in my throat I uttered, "Good bye Adam."

He died a few hours later.

I sat on the lawn at Adam's funeral and thought how I had lost a big brother…a friend…a mentor…and inspiration. Adam was the one that taught me how to race. Adam was also the one that taught me the hustle and bustle of life. He was the one that offered to take me in when I had gotten kicked out of Dave's house.

I looked across the road of the cemetery and saw my mom's grave a few thousand feet away.

I missed my mom.

I missed Adam.

My friend JD sat next to me in a numb daze as we watch the hundreds of people pay their last respects to Pierce and his family.

I saw Adam's pregnant girlfriend and thought about how her son would never know who is daddy was. In my soul I swore that I would honor "The Highlighter" someway, perhaps with a book called Heaven's Highlighter. Something. Anything. I couldn't let my friend die in vain.

After Brian Deegan rode wheelies down the cemetery concrete in honor of our fallen friend the Highlighter, we all headed to Adam's parent's house for the wake. Everyone there was numb and withdrawn. I had written a poem for Adam and passed it out to everyone.

THE SMILE

Amongst the chaos there's no denial,
That under Adam's helmet there was a smile.
Busting out a superman seat grab eighty feet in the air,
There was always a smile beneath his neon yellow hair.

With a grin from ear to ear,
Pierce made the crowd cheer.
With a smile he won the nation,
Even with his infamous **stare** of concentration.

He highlighted the show with everything he had,
He was always cheered on by his friends,
His fans and his dad.
It's hard to move on when you're still in denial,
But life seems easier when you think of Pierces' smile.

Adam's dad Ron came up to me and hugged me thanking me for such a lovely poem.

"You know John," Ron said with a sad nearly weeping voice, "Adam thought highly of you. I remember when the two of you would just ride around the fields, and," Ron's voice cracked, "and you both had so much fun together."

The moment became thick with a mournful sadness, as I said nearly choked up, "I know. Adam was like a big brother to me."

Ron nodded and agreed. He tried to say something, but instead, all he could do was squeeze my shoulder and look at me with his deep brown sad eyes, then he walked away.

It's interesting how you never know how your actions will affect people. Although I had written the poem just for Adam's family, the Highlighter must've seen this from Heaven, and spread those seeds across the world and into everyone's heart.

A few months later, JD gave me an excited call, "Dude, I saw your poem in the magazine, that's sweet!"

"What? What magazine?"

I guess there had been an editor of a dirt bike magazine at Adam's funeral, and he was touched by the poem enough that he created a full page tribute to Adam with my poem penned along the side with a photo of a rider doing a big trick into the sunset. I was honored.

But the biggest honor was when Ron called me up and asked for my "permission" to have the poem etched on Adam's tombstone.

"Would you mind?" Ron asked.

I didn't even have to think about it. "Are you kidding? That'd be the biggest eternal honor ever. Of course."

So now, when I go out to Adam's grave, I look down at the picture of his smile and read the poem, and know that my writing and his tombstone will be together for as long as this planet keeps on spinning.

That's when I really began to understand the power of the printed word, and how I truly wanted to become what I felt I was destined to be...*A Writer*.

CHAPTER
THIRTY SEVEN

"The Book Of Moser 1001..."

In September of 2002, I was crashing a creative writing class at the community college in Bakersfield. Being rebellious and somewhat cheap, or rather, more on the poor side, I decided that I'd just go to all the classes, do all the work, but just not pay or bother to enroll. My thought was, "I'm going to school for the experience, I don't care about fulfilling society's demanded obligation for a higher education."

Sounds revolutionary, right?

Sure.

As I was carousing down the campus corridors on my way to class, coming from the opposite end of the hall, was a dopey looking guy with a big nose, ape shaped teeth and stone blue eyes, wearing a backwards Broncos hat to cover his gorilla black hair and headphones covering his little monkey shaped ears. He seemed to be walking in rhythm to the music, with his hands clasped against his chest holding onto the straps of his back pack.

He seemed to be a mellow ripple in life's watery pond. As my ripple of destiny coincided with his, a changing wave, capable of inspiring a generation was the result.

It's amazing how you meet life altering friends in the most strangely coincidental way. I met Moser as we both reached the door to class at the same time. His hands on his back pack straps, my hands either in my pocket or picking my nose, we both looked at a letter on the door which said that class was cancelled.

I looked at him, he looked at me.

He shrugged his shoulders.

I smirked.

"Ah, that's too bad," he said sarcastically. "I wanted to see what kind of scarf the teacher was going to wear today."

I laughed at his keen observation and smarted, "Oh darn, no fashion show today."

Then I shrugged my shoulders.

He smirked.

And instantly our souls had been united through universal sarcasm.

We turned in unison and began traveling down the same path of life.

"So how do you like the class," I asked him.

He shrugged his shoulders and got a goofy grin, "I don't know, how *do you* like trying to write as the fifty year old teacher is switching out her silk scarves and mutating her face with make up two inches thick."

"Oh, are you jealous because you can't put your make up on in class too?" I stabbed him back with sarcasm.

"Yeah," he says swiftly, "It's sucks having to take off the clown makeup every morning after a long night of drinking whiskey and falling down in bars in the middle of the night."

"Oh, you're in the circus too? What a coincidence!" I say smiling my salesman smile.

He grunts and laughs at the same time and says, "Yeah, I thought you looked like the fat lady's boyfriend."

"Oh, Zing!" I zung.

By the time we had bombarded each other with sarcastic insults and reached the parking lot, I handed him some Dickweed stickers and told him that I was going to be president some day.

"Dickweed for President, huh?" He shrugged his smirk. "God I hope you're not a Republican bastard like Bush!"

Intrigued by his obvious political disgust for the non-Democrat president I said, "Eww, not a Bush fan huh?"

He squirmed with repressed sarcasm.

"I can't really support a President running off of daddy's coattails who likes to blow stuff up for the sake of oil and money."

"Hmm," I said, "I never thought of it that way."

He shook his head as he put the stickers in his backpack, "I don't know…there's just too much to say…guess I'll have to write about it."

"Yeah, writing is the best way to get things done," I said. "What do you think of the creative writing class so far?"

He shifted his shoulders skyward and smiled softly, "Uh, it's alright. It's my first writing class since moving from Arizona a few months ago. I moved in with my parents and they're footin' the bill for me to go to class, so, I guess I'll have to stick with it, even though the teacher is more interested in what kind of scarf and earrings she's gonna wear, instead of what she's gonna teach us."

Then, I thought quickly; "So, you live with your parents, huh?"

"Yeah."

"Well, I just got an apartment a few months ago, and I need a roommate, would you be interested?"

His eyes darted away as he thought, "Uh, sure. I'm not used to living with my parents," he said, "I want to get a place of my own. I'll think about it and I'll let you know next week."

As he said this, his girlfriend Sonja pulled up in her white 1960's Volkswagen bus, then he shook my hand and said, "Well, my chick is here, I gotta go, but I'll get some things together and see about moving in."

"Cool," I said, as he walked away to Sonja's white little bus as it sputtered and backfired. I laughed to myself and couldn't help but think that he was the classic writer; simple, sarcastic, able to survive on nothing but pen and paper...and that's how I met Eric Moser.

The next week I got a call from Moser and he said that things looked good about moving in. After class that following Tuesday, I took him to my apartment and showed him the setup. We walked up three flights of stairs, stepping carefully up all 38 steps to my second story apartment, angled at the edge of the complex, overlooking the eastern golden foothills of Bakersfield.

He got to the top of the stairs slightly short of breath and smarted, "Damn, thought I was walking up the Great Wall of China."

"Nah," I shot back sarcastically as I unlocked the door, "The Great Wall of East Bakersfield."

He laughed.

We stepped into the apartment and I gave him the tour. "This is the bathroom…this is the kitchen…this is the living room…this is my room…and this would be your room…" I say this without actually walking around with him, because it's an apartment and all of it can be seen without actually walking around.

He bobbed his head, his headphones strapped behind his neck, his thumbs through the sides of his back pack, and he said, "Alright…I'll move in."

A few weeks passed and finally Moser made his move from his parent's house and into our new writing hub, and that, is where history was made.

We'd stay up at all hours of the night discussing everything from writing, to religion, to drinking, to the purpose of life…all of which intertwined with the other…kind of like the catholic-alcoholic-writing-monk that spent a life time in a cave writing the words for all of humanity.

When I first met Moser, I considered myself a person that could write, but Moser, actually called himself a writer.

"I can't imagine living the suburban life of simplicity…holding down a nine-to-five job, mowing the grass and getting the mail…I have to write." He'd say, "It's in my blood…my soul."

I would nod my head as we each sat on the edge of the kitchen counter at three in the morning, drinking our twelfth beer.

Moser was a deep thinker and the most well read person I have ever encountered. He would start most of his conversations like; "Hunter Thompson once wrote…" then he'd quote him

word for word, or he'd say, "C.S. Lewis wrote such and such," or, "In the Bible, Paul said…"

I'd sit there, on the edge of the counter, with the little dim microwave light shining in on our conversations, and I'd listen. I personally had read maybe 10 books all the way through, and most of them were Dr. Seuss books, so to hear him quote these great larger-than-life and mysterious writers as if he knew them personally, left me in awe.

"You know John," he'd say, "Writing is eternal…think about it. All of these writers throughout the ages and for thousands of years would be nothing but a name on a tombstone somewhere in the ground."

Then he'd point his finger in a very matter of fact kind of way and say, "But their words…ah, yes, their words have lived forever! Shakespeare would just be another box of bones in a graveyard, but, because of his words, he lives everyday, in so many people's minds and souls…ah, yes, writing is eternal."

I'd nod my head and listen, then say the most wise thing I could think of, something like, "I've gotta pee…want another beer?"

"Nah," he'd say. "It's time for the whiskey." Then I'd make my way to the bathroom and he'd make his way to the porch where he'd pee off of it and into the neighbor's yard, while he smoked a cigarette and **stare**d poetically at the silent moon rising above the Eastern Bakersfield Mountains.

No doubt, Moser became my muse. I saw Moser as a writer…an alcoholic one at that, but, depending on whom you ask, they go hand-in-hand.

As four in the morning would call my wearied soul to sleep, he'd say goodnight, then as I would go to bed, he'd go to work, walking over to his little brown desk looking out the window covered with quotes from famous writers, and he'd pull out a bottle of Wild Turkey Whiskey and his little brown leather bound journal, and then he'd write until the sun came up…

When we weren't working as restaurant rats, slinging dishes for dollars and prostituting our personalities for pennies, we'd sit in our second story apartment and write words that we were sure would one day change the world.

I had been writing my "memoir-self-indulgent-what-

you're-reading-now" type of book for the past two years at that point, and Moser would sit at his desk on the opposite side of the living room. He would write his philosophical political rants about how the country and the soul of society was surely going to hell from its lack of introspection.

I would type tenaciously at my computer and he'd scribble in his leather note books for hours.

"Here, read this," I'd say, printing out a page and handing it to him.

"Here, read this," he'd say, handing me his journal.

We'd read for a few minutes then come back into a lengthy beer fueled discussion how we were quite possibly the greatest writers of our generation and how we, yes we, were going to change the hearts, minds and souls of all the people whom we'd never meet. We discussed how we single handily would provide salvation and hope for the lost and mentally disturbed.

"I don't know," he'd say as he would begin with what he did "in fact" know. "We have this ability to write the things that millions of people like us feel, but can't articulate. Shit, man, we can do so much."

Then I'd chime in, "Yet we do so little."

"I don't know man," he'd say again, "I'm getting tired running around a restaurant and sucking someone's ass for a five dollar tip….I don't know about you, but I just want to write."

I'd nod my head and smirk, then shrug my trademark shoulders. "Yeah, I'm tired of people asking me at the tables, 'So, what are you doing with you life?', then they look at me expectantly and I say, 'I'm going to be a writer that will one day change the world!' and they just look at me blankly like I'm an ambitious idiot. Then they say, 'Oh, you want to be poor all your life, eh?' I just want to punch them in the face and stand on their table while I beat my chest and say, 'I am a writer! Read my words!'"

Moser would laugh, and I would chuckle at my out of control egotistical ranting and raving.

"Well," I say, "It *could* happen."

"Yeah," he'd say, "And monkeys could fly out my ass and vote Republican."

"Hmm," I'd think, "Good point."

CHAPTER
THIRTY EIGHT

PLAN: To put on a Christian Motocross freestyle dirt bike exhibition near the baseball field at Valley Bible Fellowship on **February 16, 2002.**

PURPOSE: This event will serve several purposes, all reflecting the glory of God.
1). Glorify God through praise of His accomplishing this event.
2). To promote the Christian Motocross Ministry.
3). Increase attendance at Valley Bible Fellowship.
4). Introduce people from the motorcycle community to Valley Bible.
5). To gain exposure for Valley Bible and CMX through a live radio broadcast from KDUV 100.1 fm

PROCEDURE: After six weeks of effectively promoting the event through announcements, bulletins, and other forms of advertising, the CMX crew will set up the exhibition site. The site will be 150' long by 75' wide (site ~~can be altered for space regulations). We have (2) eight foot ramps that~~

"Putting the Cross in MotoCROSS..."

By the time December drifted through a field of Bakersfield fog, we became a bit more grounded and spiritual. I had been going faithfully to Valley Bible Fellowship, and my faith in Christ was beginning to be the focus of my life and future.

One morning, three days after Christmas, as Moser's friends from Arizona were sleeping in a stoned daze on our apartment floor, I walked outside to our porch with my Bible and morning coffee and began to do my daily Bible study.

As I was reading my devotion for the day, I began to feel an immense spiritual presence from God Himself, and began having visions within my mind and soul about doing a youth focused dirt bike ministry. I started scribbling down all these intense impressions in my notebook.

In my soul, I envisioned gathering a group of riders together, namely my friend JD, who had recently got out of a youth correctional institution with a changed heart and purpose of serving God. So I thought of creating this group which would be called Christian Motocross, or CMX for short. As a group, I saw that we could have an immense impact upon the riding community as we would ride and pray together, encouraging others to ride the narrow path to heaven and to hope.

Along with the rider's group which would serve as a motocross ministry, I also felt God leading me to start a youth center in downtown Oildale, which was known more for its drug use, trailer parks and a run down sense of life and spiritual purpose. My mind began to race with clear visions of exactly what building to rent, who to talk to and how it would all be done. In my heart, I heard the Holy voice of God saying, "Do this…and I will be with you."

Excited and full of the Spirit, I waited for Moser to wake up so I could share this with him. When he awoke groggy eyed and slightly sleepy, I jumped at him with my notebook and went in depth about all that had happened in my heart that morning.

As I finished with a fanatical look upon my face, he **stare**d at me, rubbed his eyes and then calmly said, "Cool."

"Cool?" I said taken back by his lack of complete joy and enthusiasm, "This is the greatest thing that will ever happen! Will you be apart of it?"

He yawned and stretched as he looked in our refrigerator and saw nothing but a pizza box with a single slice in it. Then he picked up the pizza, took a bite and said, "Sure."

I continued on creating flyers and information about Christian Motocross and called people I thought should be involved. Later in the day, Moser finally came to me and said, "John, I've been thinking about the whole CMX deal in Oildale. I think that's something I want to do. It'd be a great way to get back to what Christianity should really be about, helping others in need. I want to do this."

"Yes!" I said, finally satisfied with his agreement. Then we discussed providing food and clothing for the less fortunate, and how we could really get this thing started.

I wasn't sure how things were going to be funded, but I just started trusting that God would provide something. A few days later, as I was doing my daily devotional, I got another inspiring insight for funding the entire project: Raffling off a 2003 KTM 125 dirt bike.

The plan would be to sell raffle tickets for $5 and use that money to pay for the building and supplies. Sounds awesome, right?

Just wait and see…

Moser and I drove over to the Oildale building and noticed that it was for rent. I pulled into the parking lot that paralleled N. Chester Avenue, and we parked the van in front of the building.

"This is it!" I shouted with a child like smile.

Moser got out of the van and rubbed his hands together to warm them up, then looked at me with his hazel blue eyes beneath his beanie and said, "This is it?"

I looked at the 500 square foot building, then back at him and said proudly, "Yep, this is it!"

He puckered his lips pessimistically to the side and then shrugged his shoulders nodding his head and said, "It looks like a big blue and white shoe box."

I scowled, feeling as though he had just called me ugly or had just kicked my dog, then I told him, "It's not much, but it's only $500 a month."

He looked at the building again, then at me and said, "Hell, I have a few shoe boxes in my closet I'll rent you for that much."

Moser eventually became enthusiastic about our $500 shoe box as we called the owner of the building to discuss renting it. When the owner showed up, we thought a gang of bikers would soon be following him in.

The owner's name was Butch and he was an ex-Hell's Angel with demonic tattoos covering his arms and body and around his neck. I went to shake his hand and noticed that he had "Love" tattooed across his right knuckles and "Hate" tatted across his left knuckles. I made sure to shake his right hand.

Butch unlocked the door then looked at us beneath his black bandana and asked, "So what you boys want with a building like this."

Moser gave me a strange look when I **stare**d at him as if to say, *'Go ahead, and tell him…this'll be interesting.'*

I looked at Butch and cleared my throat, "Well, Mr. Butch, sir, uh, um, we actually wanna start a youth center here for the kids of the neighborhood. You know, like an after school hang out where kids can be around a good positive environment, and play games and do Bible studies and things like that."

Butch petted his foot long gray goatee, then scowled and repeated back like a parrot getting his feathers pulled, "B*ib*le studies?!"

Moser looked at me and smirked. I stood still, unsure what Butch was thinking. Butch **stare**d at me while I **stare**d at a faded black tattooed demon on his forearm standing in a pulpit with a decapitated priest's head in its mouth. Instantly I felt that we were a little out of place.

Butch twisted his chin hair and suspiciously eyed the two of us. "Can ya'll pay rent?"

Moser raised his eye brows, again, prompting me to answer.

"Uh, yes sir, Mr. Butch, sir." I said still swimming around in my skin.

Butch turned around and continued walking around the building showing us its features, "Well I reckon if you boys gots da money, I don't really give a dog damn what'ch'all do with it."

Moser smiled.

I felt relieved.

We looked around the square building which was separated front and back by a big white wall about twenty five feet long. The carpet was a brand new electric blue color and all the walls had just been painted with a fresh coat of white. The bathroom was the size of a small closet and it had a small storage room for supplies the size of a pantry.

"Well, whad'ya'll think?" Butch asked.

I smiled my salesman smile, Moser smirked, and I stretched out my hand, making sure that it was my *right* one, and said, "We'll take it."

(JD McCaslin, John, Jerret McCaslin & Joe Shroeder, CMX promotion at Valley Bible)

Now that we had the building and a $500 dollar a month obligation, we began setting a booth up outside of Valley Bible showing off the KTM 125. JD and the riders showed up wearing their FLY gear, which had been sponsored to us as a surprise blessing, and we handed out flyers to the church's some 5,000 members. People were buying dozens of raffle tickets and things were going good.

In February, we had sold a few hundred dollars of raffle tickets and we paid our first month's rent. We went to the Taft Grand Prix where JD was racing, and sold $800 worth of tickets...we were all getting excited.

Although things were going good, Moser and I were starting to feel the pressure of making sure things were moving forward. We would meet Bob every week for lunch and Jake's Tex Mex, where we would sit out at the park and listen to his wisdom beneath towering trees.

Moser and I had a fly-by-the-seat-of-your-pants kind of faith, but Bob, being much older and wiser, and more logical and practical, would advise us of what we were getting ourselves into.

"So," Bob would say in between bites of his chicken sandwich. "How are you guys going to staff the place?"

Moser would shrug, and I would smirk, then I'd answer and say, "Well, I guess we'll take turns."

Bob would chew his food while he thought about the technicalities of running such a place, "Well, have you guys checked on things like fire codes and insurance?"

Moser and I would hang our heads and say no.

Bob would think some more and say, "Have you thought about how you're going to pay for the bills like electricity and water?"

Again, we'd hang our heads and say no.

By the end of lunch, Bob would reaffirm us that we were indeed trying to do a good thing for the community, but he'd also reiterate that there were a lot of loose ends that we would have to take care of.

Bob would take out his glasses from his shirt pocket and would read us the Bible verse about the foolish man that built his house on the sand, and the wise man that built his house on a rock.

Moser and I would **stare** at each other as the reality of our responsibility began to sink in. After Bob read the passage, he took off his glasses, slid them back into his shirt pocket and asked, "So, are you guys building a house in the sand or on a rock?"

Moser and I shrugged our shoulders, shook our heads side-to-side and admitted that we were probably building it in some really wet mud.

Bob would look at us with wisdom and support and say, "I believe in you guys, just keep doing what you think God is telling you to do. Just make sure you're doing it for the right reasons."

By the beginning of March, the stress of paying for another month's rent was really upon us. JD and the other riders began to draw a line in the sand stating that they didn't really want to do the whole building youth center thing, they just wanted to ride and do freestyle shows. The building was more of my and Moser's passion and the riders didn't want to be apart of it. Already, the ministry was beginning to separate.

Regardless, I proceeded to publish more flyers for an upcoming event that JD was going to be doing. It was March 2nd and a friend of ours was putting on a freestyle motocross show out in a bull riding arena south of town. The plan was JD would ride in the event as a CMX rider and I, along with Moser and some others, would set up a booth and sell raffle tickets and t-shirts.

On the day of the event, we showed up early and hung up CMX posters everywhere. In the middle of the bull ring, the promoter had built a landing ramp with the take off ramp about sixty feet back. Steel stands surrounded the small ring, and people began to show up in herds.

The motocross scene in Bakersfield people were really into the Metal Mulisha, which was a popular riding group that Adam Pierce was a part of, and because of Pierce and his legendary status around his hometown of Bakersfield, people were into being *hardcore*.

Most of the riders wore black shirts and pants, and were into flipping off the crowd being as punk rock as they could. JD on the other hand, was dressed in his colorful FLY gear, and he'd ride with an enthusiastic attitude, encouraging the crowd with his positive presence.

The atmosphere of the event was awkward. People would walk by our booth somewhat cold and distant. Families and friends on the other hand, were really supportive of us and bought shirts and such.

As the event wore on through the day, JD put on an awesome show and became the focal point of all the fans in the stands. People were coming up to him and getting autographs, and JD loved every minute of it.

(JD McCaslin in style at CMX event)

Later that night, as we were watching the Channel 17 news, the newscasters did a segment on the motocross event. But, the only rider they showed was JD doing all his crazy tricks, completely neglecting the dozen or so negative riders because they were flipping off the crowd and acting drunk.

Instantly, CMX became the hot buzz around town.

People were calling us up the next day claiming they saw CMX on the news and they wanted to be a part of it.

JD and the riders were excited, but Moser and I still had to worry about the paying for rent the next day for the building.

After reviewing the finances, which were only a few hundred dollars in the bank, and realizing that we still had to pay for the $5,000 dirt bike, before we could actually use any of the money (which we already were). I became frustrated and was about to call up Butch, the building's landlord, and tell him that we weren't going to be able to pay for the month of March.

Moser was lying in his room as I popped my head in and said, "Well, unless a miracle happens, I don't think we can continue on with the building."

Moser looked at me through the stressed shadows of his room and nodded his head, "Yeah, well, we tried…at least we had it for a month."

I walked back to my desk and was about to pick up the phone to call Butch with the news, when suddenly…the phone rang.

I answered it, "Hello?"

The voice on the other end of the phone was raspy and excited, like a smoker who smoked for twenty years and had just found a carton of cigarettes under the couch, "Hello, hello, oh man, is this CMX?"

My eyebrows narrowed, "Yes it is, can I help you?"

Again, the man's voice seemed excited and eccentric and echoed with electricity, "Oh, geez, man, I don't even know where to start. My family and I were at the event yesterday and we saw that JD kid ride and boy o' boy, my kids love him!"

I smiled against the mouth piece of the phone, "Oh, that's great."

The man tried to calm himself down, "Yeah, yeah, well I got one of your flyers and saw what ya'll are up to, and how you guys are doing a youth center and all that, man, O, man, I think you guys really got something going there! I want to be a part of this, I want to be the financer, I'll back you guys up with all the money ya'll need, pay for everything! My wife and I are just so excited about this Christian ministry, it's just what the motocross scene needs here in town! I couldn't even sleep last night, I's so excited!"

I thought to myself that I must be dreaming; did he really just say that he wanted to *pay* for *everything*?

"Well, that sounds great," I said. "How bout we meet?"

Then his raspy voice raced, "Oh yes, yes, yes…definitely yes! I want to get the ball rolling right away. This thing is going to be huge!"

I got his name and told him to meet us at our Oildale building, so Moser and I could meet him and show him our plans for the property.

When I hung up the phone, I went into Moser's shadowy room and stuck my head in and said, "You'll never believe what just happened!"

He lifted his head from the pillow and his eyes widened expectedly, "What?!"

"Some guy just called and wants to be the financier for the entire ministry…wants to pay for the building and buy new bikes for the riders and everything!"

Moser's face remained straight, obviously speechless, "Shut up!" he finally said in disbelief.

He jumped out of bed as I told him about a guy named George McChristian who just called and wanted to meet with us to discuss all the plans.

"Oh man," Moser shook his head, "So God's still in the miracle business."

I shrugged my shoulders and couldn't help but feel like a divine intervention had just occurred.

Despite this last minute excitement that this was perhaps the answer to all our prayers, I should've listened the small voice in the softness of my spirit warn me and say; *'Beware of easy blessings...wolves may come in sheep's clothing.'*

Moser and I galloped down the thirty eight stairs of our second story apartment and sped off in my van to our ministry building.

As we drove along 7th Standard Road amidst the drilling oil refineries, we couldn't help but feel like we had just struck it rich.

"This can mean so much," Moser said staring out the window with refreshed enthusiasm about our proposed project.

"We can put that skate ramp in and you and the kids can skate like how you wanted!" I spoke with a wild imagination and fast tone.

When we got to the building, George was already standing there with his arms crossed looking at the building. I parked the van in front of the sidewalk and **stare**d at the short and stocky man. Somehow, the voice seemed to match the body; he had a walrus like mustache and ashy blonde color, and his plump red face seemed squeezed with hyper active stress.

I introduced myself and Moser to George, and when he started talking his tough tracker sounding voice thundered and crackled through his two missing bottom teeth.

"Oh guys, this is awesome! Just wait until we get'r goin'," George said. "My wife and I have been waiting for a Christian thing like this, look, look here, see my business card, it has a dove on it and my name is McChristian, almost like its meant to be, huh?"

I looked to Moser to laugh, but I noticed he had an uneasy smile and a suspicious look in his eyes, as he nodded his head.

"Now listen guys, I don't wanna step on ya'll's toes, I just want to be the financial overseer, ya know, I pay the bills and ya'll just keep doing what'cha'll been doin'."

I seemed eager to agree with that, because all of the financial aspects had been my responsibility, and it was beginning to be tiresome and stressful. Figuring this guy called in the final hour before I was about to give up, made me think that this was God's way of providing somebody in the nick of time.

I felt relieved of my responsibility, but, especially after the look in Moser's eye, I could tell in my soul that something just didn't seem right.

George was intent on meeting with the other CMX members, so I told him they were probably riding behind JD's dad's tractor trailer shop out in Rosedale.

George was anxious to go meet with them, so he took off to Rosedale and said he'd meet with us later after he got the full scope on what was going on with everybody in the group.

Moser and I drove back to the apartment, smiling and driving. Moser seemed a bit more serious; his demeanor distant and quiet.

"What's up man, aren't you excited about all this?" I jolted him with a quick jab to the arm.

He pinched his lips in his typical pessimistic way and continued to think. "I don't know man," he said with an uncertain voice. "Don't you think that all this is a bit, I don't know, weird?"

"Of course it's weird," I stated. "God always works in mysterious ways!"

He shrugged his unsure shoulders, "I don't know man…remember the other day when we were reading about the wolf in sheep's clothing? How people can step in what seems to be just the right time, with all this money and everything that we need, I can't help but wonder if this is the devil's way of deceit somehow."

I looked at him, not really wanting to believe that this blessing could somehow be a curse, "No way, man. This is a total answered prayer!"

Again he shrugged stiffly and suspiciously and said "We'll see."

Well, Moser was right. His cynical attitude had some aptitude to it, because three weeks later I found myself sitting on the green church lawn staring at the sunset, waiting to be called in by my pastor.

George McChristian, within three weeks, got into the middle of the ministry and began separating everybody, convincing them that if they followed his lead, that everything would be better.

He said it to me and Moser.

He said it to JD and riders.

He even said it to JD's mom.

Soon, we had all become deceived that handing him control of the ministry would be in "God's" best interest.

The dirt bike raffle had become a financial issue for the ministry, as George began riling up negative reactions from people saying that, "It was a legal liability because we didn't actually have the bike, so if someone wanted to sue us for selling raffle tickets for something that wasn't ours, then they could."

George had called a meeting with the pastor of my church deceptively behind my back, as he had JD try to have me hand over all the money of the ministry. I heard JD on the phone with George, and because George talked so loudly, I heard his plan and decided to intercept.

I drove over to Valley Bible and saw George and JD's mom Genevive walking into the pastor's office. George was planning on discrediting me with out my presence, telling my pastor that I was trying to cause legal problems for the church and what not, and George wasn't thrilled to see that I was there.

My pastor, a wise man with a caring heart and a logical mind, met with George and Genevive first, and told me to wait outside.

So, outside I waited, staring into the swirling clouds and the setting sun. I was absolutely baffled that one phone call from a stranger offering money just three weeks before, had boiled down to me losing the motocross ministry that I felt so certain God had called me to do.

With a heavy heart and a saddened spirit, I prayed to God that all of this would happen for a reason. I wanted to cry, but crying, as you've read, was hard to come by. All I could do was sit there and pray for God's grace and deliverance.

When the pastor called me in, George was sitting in a chair with his arms crossed and an evil glare at me, like, *Ha! I got your ministry.*

Instantly, I thought back to Moser saying how wolves can come in sheep's clothing. I felt that my ministry had been infiltrated by the devil himself.

In the end, my pastor said that the church was going to buy the motorcycle and finish off the raffle. He suggested that I step aside from the ministry, and just let it go and leave it up to God.

It's not what I wanted to hear, but, in the end, I figured God knew what was best, and perhaps that meant that I'd have to offer up the ministry in order for something better to happen. George insisted that JD and the riders should still ride for him, but, I heard later that the ministry fell apart a few days later, and soon, George was nowhere to be found.

The flock had scattered, and the wolf had made off with a few sheep.

CHAPTER
THIRTY NINE

(Creative consultant Moser)

"Is this the highest plain for me?..."

Back at the apartment, Moser and I slumped into a few week blur of binge drinking. Moser had problems with the church before the ministry, but during the ministry it seemed as though his faith had been reinvigorated. But now, we felt like we had been beat up in the spiritual realm, so we just sat on the couch, drank our beer and watched *The Simpsons* through a cloud of smoke and confusion.

As if things weren't going downhill spiritually, at the end of May, as I was serving tables at Carrows, I got a call from my girlfriend at the time, her voice sad and crying, "John, Moser's friend was killed in a car accident."

I dropped the phone and fell to my knees. Moser's friend Joe Pealstrom, the lead singer of the stoner band Herb-n-Life, had come out a few months before from Arizona to visit us, and today was to be the same. We had gotten a call early that morning from Joe on our answering machine saying that he was on his way out to see us. When Moser played the message, he got excited and was ready for a night of partying with Joe.

But now, Joe was dead.

And, in a sense, so was Moser.

I rushed out of the restaurant and pulled into the parking lot of the apartment, and ran up the 38 steps of stairs to our place. When I walked in, I saw Moser's chick Sonja standing in the small hallway holding her arms sadly to herself.

"Where's Moser?" I asked short of breath.

She pointed to the balcony.

I walked over the sliding screen door, and slid it aside and took a seat next to Moser. He had his hands folded against his chin, his **stare** distant and dead.

The silence was thick and saturated with sadness, and then I placed my hand on his shoulder and said, "Let it out, man. Just cry and let it out."

Before I finished saying that, he began shuddering and crying from the depths of his soul. Joe was like a little brother to Moser, like I was to Adam Pierce. I knew how Moser was feeling in that moment and I knew he just had to cry and let the pain go.

We spent the night confused and crying. Later, Sonja drove him to Arizona to be with his friends out there for the funeral.

When Moser came back from Arizona, he was quiet and withdrawn. If he wasn't working, he was in his room sleeping all day or drinking whisky straight from the bottle. The entire summer became this same dried and dead routine of sleeping, working and drinking.

My girlfriend Sarah, the girl that I had been with for the past three years during most of my trials and tribulations, had come to the point that she was 19 and wanted to experience life on her own level…without me. As I have written this book, I decided not to include much about her, because the relationship was always rocky and full of resentments, but now that she wanted to be on her own, I found myself alone in my apartment.

The summer of 2003 was becoming worse. Not only had I lost the ministry that I had worked hard to build, but I lost my girlfriend and my job. Actually, I guess I didn't lose it (as if I could find it again or something) but, because of the stress of everything, I decided to walk out in the middle of the dinner rush.

My life was falling apart like a house built on sand (or really wet mud as I had once said), and Moser as well began having relationship problems with Sonja. Within six months, our lives had gone from prospering in the ministry, to a crumbling house of cards.

I sat on the couch across from Moser with a twelve pack and a bottle of Whisky between us, and we began to reflect on how we had once stood atop our stairs in front of the apartment, and how we used to pray for God to give us strength.

"You know," Moser said. "When you pray for God to give you strength, He doesn't just give it to you…He breaks you down into little pieces until you can barely stand it, then He rebuilds you into a strength that comes from nearly nothing. That's how God works."

I **stare**d at the bottle of Whisky and thought of taking a slug, but felt that any more would just leave me with a headache and a sour stomach, then I said, "If I knew that this was going to happen, I would've just prayed for a puppy."

Moser laughed. Then he slammed a shot of Whisky and winced. "I don't know," he said, and as he always did, he followed up with what he did know. "I just think that God has a bigger plan than us just renting a building in Oildale and trying to sell the ministry through t-shirts and stickers, maybe this is what God wanted?"

Moser stared at his hands as a slow acoustic strumming song of Joe's, *'Is this the Highest Plain for me?'*, was playing through our speakers.

> *I'm tired of waiting*
> *I'm tired of waiting*
> *My feet are tied down*
> *And I'm so frustrated*
> *Is this the highest plain for me?*
> *Will it ever be?*

Looking around the small apartment, I saw the posters of Alfred Hitchcock and other movies, and cut out pages of my book samples hanging on the walls.

"I just want to be a writer," I told Moser.

His eyes lifted up to mine as he nodded. "You will man. You just gotta keep at it. Keep writing. Your book is coming along, you just need to finish it when God tells you its done, then get it published and do your thing, ya know?"

I got a deep and distant **stare** in my eyes as I nodded. My book had become my refuge. When all else had failed in my life, I figured that it would all make a great story one day, and that story would be in my book or in some other book. But as optimistic as I wanted to be, I couldn't help but feel like it was all just some far off dream…a dream that would never happen.

Moser must've noticed that I was doubting myself when he said, "I believe in you John. Everything happens for a reason, you know that. Everything with your mom and Adam, and the drugs and stuff you went through, hell, even this ministry, its all gonna be a good story someday. You just keep living the life that God has called you to live, and you write about it. The rest is up to God."

I looked at him with hopeful eyes, but with a pessimistic shoulder shrug.

"I hope you're right Moser."

He smirked. "Well, I might not be right. But, just keep writing and see what happens."

I laughed half-heartedly, "Why don't we write a book together?"

He smiled, "Maybe we will…maybe we will."

By the time the fall leaves were falling from the tree, my life had become stuck in neutral with the drive of my soul revving, but the destination driving nowhere. I was working in another restaurant running around like a rat trying to earn nothing more than cheese, when one day I got a two-way call from my Aunt Mary in Boston with my Nana on the other line.

"J-awn," my aunt's accented voice came through. "I was thinking a-bouwt you the otha day, and I th-ouwght you'd likes to come to Boston over the h-owli-days to come and stay."

I held the phone to my ear and slightly laughed at her accent that I loved so much. Looking around my apartment, I couldn't help but feel that my life wasn't going anywhere fast, and perhaps this was some sort of spiritual intervention.

Then my Nana, also from Massachusetts, chimed in, "Yeah, J-awn, maybe you could go stay with A-awnt M-awhry and then you could come to Temecula and live here with Red and I, and go to school…You wouldn't have to pay rent, just go to school and get a job down here."

But could I really move to the east coast for six weeks, Thanksgiving through New Years?

Hmm, it was tempting…however, our lease was ending at the end of November, and Moser had mentioned that he was thinking about moving back with his parents before possibly moving to Los Angeles to go to school.

But it was a dramatic change…should I?…could I?…would I?

Hmmm….

"Okay," I said. "When would I leave?"

And, after a few minutes of discussion, my destiny and path of life was about to change forever…

CHAPTER
FORTY

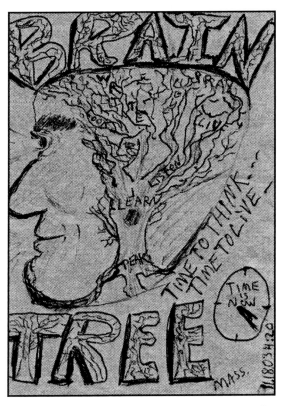

"Braintree..."

When I landed in the Massachusetts airport, I was met by my Aunt and Uncle, Mary and Dick. Mary was short and stocky with blonde straight hair and deep blue eyes. Dick, who I would end up calling Dicky Boy, was about five foot tall, and well, about five foot round, with hysterical blue pug shaped eyes and slightly balding. Mary was sweet and spiritual, and good ole Dicky Boy was just like Archy Bunker.

Immediately, I became enthralled with these two new characters as they drove me from the airport and to their house in Braintree, just 10 miles from Boston.

"These damned zippah heads!" My Uncle Dick shouted as he drove their mini-van through a crowd of what he considered to be "less than humanly equipped to drive a car" traffic.

"Oh Dicky, s-tawp it!" My Aunt Mary said.

When we got to their small two story house, they showed me my room. It was a small room with a slanted wall and wooden floors. A simple single sized bed with a computer desk and a set of dresser drawers with a huge picture of Mother Teresa that my devout Catholic Aunt Mary had painted.

I unloaded my bags full of my clothes, my laptop, and my Bible. Just the necessities, as I had left most of my belongings back in Bakersfield at Bob's house. Bob was sad to see me leave Bakersfield, but he too felt that God was calling me on a journey of self and spiritual discovery.

"Go there and be a shining light to all those you meet," Bob had written in a card stuffed with $200. "I love you and believe in you…God has a plan for your life."

I already missed Bob and Bakersfield, but I knew within my heart that God had brought me 2,000 miles away to discover something deeper.

The first few days on the east coast were filled with sleep due to the jetlag. When I was awake, Mary and I would talk about my book and my life in Bakersfield.

"So, J-awn," she would say, pronouncing my name with her Bostonian accent. "How's your book coming a-lowng?"

Mary was the first person that read my stuff, back in Ortega almost two years before, and she was insistent that I work and finish my book while I was there in Boston.

I shrugged my shoulders, smirked, then said, "Uhh, I don't know. I just want to get it done. I hope to write a lot while I'm here."

She smiled supportively, then said, "You know, J-awn, God's given you a gift. You need to use it."

I'd smile and nod. "I think He has too, I just don't know when, if ever it's going to be done."

But, after our late night conversations, I would go up into my room and write. I wound up rewriting the entire first chapter of my book which dealt with hearing my Mom had a tumor from one chapter, into ten chapters. The six weeks I spent in Massachusetts became my most intimate time writing my book. Within those six weeks, I wrote eighteen chapters for my book. Compared to a chapter every few months before hand, the difference was exceptional.

While I was there, I sought after God's calling for my life. I told Him that I was open to whatever He had for me. When my cousin Lenny called and said he wanted to take me to a *Cursillo*, an exclusive weekend that dealt with Jesus alone with other like minded Christians came up, I was open for it.

"Sure, I'll go," I said happily.

"You will?" Lenny said, also with his Bostonian accent. "That's great."

That weekend was probably the most influential Christ-based weekend of my life. There, a group of 70 men spent the weekend searching for God and seeking His will for their lives. We shared stories of struggle and triumph, and by the time we left, we felt as though we had been in the presence of Christ Himself.

My outlook on life had changed, and now that my book was coming along, I felt that God was weaving all His works into my life, and into my book.

When I wasn't writing, I was hanging out downstairs with Mary and Uncle Dick. Dick would sit on his recliner and watch the Patriots try to get into the Super Bowl. I personally have never been a big sports kind of guy beside motocross, but watching his hometown passion made it contagious to watch the football game and root for the home team.

"Those damned zippah heads!" He'd shout at the refs.

I'd look at him and smile then ask, "What's a 'zippah-head'?"

He'd look at me for a quick second like I was a confused Californian, "Zippah head, you know, idiots that have a zipper on their head and their brain falls o-ouwt!"

"Oh," I'd say with a smile and a smirk.

I spent the entire holiday season on the east coast, and I couldn't help but feel that it was like a plan from God. While there, I wrote my book and searched after what I thought God was calling me to do; and that was to write.

But, during Christmas, I couldn't help but feel sad as everyone opened their gifts, and somehow I felt that I no longer had a family. I had a lot of Aunts and Uncles and Cousins, but not the traditional sense of the family as in my Mom and Dad.

I prayed that God would cure my sadness. Surprisingly the day after Christmas, my Aunt Kelly from California, unbeknownst to me, had sent me some pictures of my Mom when I was a little baby. It could've been coincidence, but I saw it as God answering my prayer as if saying, "Yes. I know you're sad without your Mom. But here you go, here are some pictures…"

When I boarded the airplane back to California on January 3rd, I felt that my time in Braintree, Massachusetts had been fulfilled. As we landed in Los Angeles, and we began to leave the plane, I heard Tom Petty's song *Wild Flowers*, playing over the speakers:

> *You belong, amongst the wild flowers,*
> *You belong, in a boat out at sea…*

That was a song that I had listened to in Ortega, when I would go out in the wild flowers with my Aunt Beth and pick Sage. I would hear hit when I'd go out on the boat with my Uncle Craig, out at sea.

The song just hit my heart in the right way and suddenly I knew that I was back on track…California was my home…my life…my place of purpose, and now that we had landed, my home life was about to begin…

CHAPTER
FORTY ONE

"When John Met Jen…"

The tables were full of lovers on a very romantic Valentine's night at an Italian restaurant where people came looking for love, looking for life, and looking for some good lasagna, too.

I had just started serving tables with smiles in January of 2004, when I found myself running around the restaurant seeking salads, and passing off pastas. Suddenly I came to the end of the expo line and saw a strawberry beauty, pleasing to the eyes and soul.

She was a preciously petite girl wearing pig tales in her strawberry blonde hair. Her face was softly drawn by heaven's most special designer, and her existence mellowed my heart with her mossy green eyes. Her soft freckled skin colored like cinnamon and cream.

I was waiting for my food when I saw her standing there in her work uniform which was a white shirt and black pants, looking flashy with a fancy colored tie. She was waiting for her food and seemed to be staring off into the warm sensual glow of the oven looking for love, looking for life and looking for her pizza, too.

With the smoothest salesman smile that I could possibly smile, I stood next to her. With all my charm and sarcastic style, I asked with a stretched suave voice, "*So0, what are yo0u and yo0ur* boyfriend doing for Valentine's tonight?"

She **stare**d at me with her gorgeous green eyes and smiled a simple comma carved dimple smile, and shrugged her shoulders softly saying, "*Oh,* I don't have a boyfriend."

I smirked stupidly, "Oh, me neither…"

If I was any smoother I probably would have winked with a special sparkle in my eye.

I spent the rest of the night running around the restaurant for lovers, serving lasagna, serving laughs, still looking across the room for love.

A few days later, I was leaving work from a lunch time shift I had served. She was sitting there on the brown benches beneath the blue sky of love and life.

I walked past her at first, but then I realized that I forgot my check in the restaurant. I returned to the building, making sure that my shoulders were pulled back and my chin was held high, you know, just in case she was watching.

When I came back out, she was still sitting there waiting for a ride, so once again in my smoothest stylish salesman voice, I asked, "SoO, what time am I picking you up for the movies tonight?"

She looked at me smiling and laughing, "Uh, gee, I don't know, you tell me."

"How about eight o'clock?" I said trying to lean casually on a wooden wall post, but nearly lost my balance and bumped my arm.

She grinned and giggled.

I cleared my throat confidently trying to regain my courage, "Uh, huh, well, yeah, like I said, eight o'clock?"

"Okay, sure." She smiled with a soft and simple romantic radiance.

Then we exchanged each other's phone numbers and in doing so, intertwined our experiences of love and life with each other, forever.

Our days of dating soon danced away the calendar pages. In Spring, we spent our days serving in the restaurant, and spending time in each other's arms by night.

Soon the Summer sizzle of passion, put us on a path up the 101 through the towering trees of the redwood valleys, overlooking the Oregon ocean, on our way to visit each other's families on vacation.

And that amazing August night against the Oregon ocean, we both **stare**d into each other's eyes and whispered those three wonderful words… ***I love you…***"

A few months later, as we were driving across the 215 overpass across the 15 freeway, with Creed's *Arms Wide Open* song playing on the radio, she looked at me from the passenger seat and asked, "Is this song about having a baby?"

I **stare**d out the windshield and saw the red stream of tail lights from the traffic, and to my left saw the white lights of the oncoming traffic. I looked over at her and said, "Yes."

She sat quiet for a moment, and as she did, my soul knew before she said anything else…I looked at her and she looked at me, then she said softly, somewhat scared and unsure, "I think I'm pregnant…"

The blessed feeling of terror and uncertainty filled my soul, as I smiled awkwardly and tried to keep the car from veering off the road. "You're pregnant?" I asked. "Are you sure?"

She nodded, still staring at me to see what I was going to do. I took a deep breath, prayed in my soul for forgiveness and strength and courage and everything else that I was going to need for the rest of my life, and then I **stare**d back at her, smiled simply, and said, "Well, I hope it's a boy."

For a few weeks my soul struggled and strained with spiritual seeking. Being a Christian, I had been convicted from the spirit as we would have our sensual nights together, but damned man that I am, I fell to my flesh every time. As the Bible says, "The spirit is willing, but the flesh is weak."

I prayed for forgiveness and found myself searching for God's grace. "God, I know I did things backwards. But Jen is the one that I love, and I'm sorry we didn't get married first, but Lord, I ask that you will give me the strength to do what is right…"

Thankfully, I already knew from our Oregon trip that Jen was the girl that I wanted to love for the rest of my life. With that as assurance, I knew that I wanted her to be my wife.

Back at the restaurant, I worked my butt off and took as many tables as I could, scraping every penny and dollar from my bank account. I went to a jewelry store and bought her a small simple shiny diamond ring.

The day we went to pick it up, it was raining, so I took Jen to the Shoe Pavilion next to the Jewelry Mart. I told her, "I need to get some work shoes...oh, dang it, I forgot my wallet in the car, can you look around and try to find some shoes for me?"

She held her arms across her stomach, trying not to get sick from the smell of the shoes, and nodded.

I ran out the door, into the rain, and next door to the jewelry mart. I paid the cashier the remaining cash that I had in my account and asked sarcastically, as I held the ring in the box, "So...if she says no, do you have a return policy?"

The cashier chuckled for a moment, then got straight faced and said, "No. Better hope she says yes."

I ran back out into the rain and placed the little black box on the passenger seat of the car, and sprinted back into the shoe store.

Jen looked pale and nauseous as I said, "Oh well. I don't really want to get any shoes from here anyway, let's go."

We walked out holding hands as the rain moistened the tops of our heads with heavenly blessing, then I opened up the door and she saw the little box.

"What's this?" She asked, as I ran over to the driver side.

"Will you marry me?" I asked her as she opened up the lid of the little box and saw the diamond ring.

She smiled, sliding the ring on her skinny finger, and said, "Yes...of course I will!"

We **stare**d at each other sensually, and kissed.

Now, my fiancé, the fun loving sarcastic beauty that she is, on our drive home from the shoe store looked at me and said, "So what? You couldn't get down on one knee?"

I smirked, "Hey! It was raining!"

She grinned, "Yeah, but on all the movies, the guy gets down on one knee."

Then I thought, and told her, "Yeah but look…how romantic am I? Shoes and diamonds are girls two favorite things, right? So I took you to a shoe store, and we left with a diamond ring!"

She laughed and sat quiet for a few moments, then said again as her final sarcastic stab, "Yeah…but you still could've gotten down on one knee."

So now, with a little baby Butler growing inside of her belly, and a ring on her finger, our family was beginning to blossom. Only now came the hardest part…telling her parents.

"I don't want to tell my mom until she comes back from Africa," Jen said slightly scared.

I thought, staring out the windshield, holding onto the steering wheel, "Why don't we just tell them now?"

She sat quietly and **stare**d at her ring, twisting it around her finger, "Because I don't want her to worry while she's in Africa."

Her mom was going to Africa on one of those safari expeditions, and her trip wasn't for another month.

"I think we should tell them now," I said, although I was scared to death in my soul about having the confronting conversation. What was I going to say, "Hey, Tom and Julie, guess what?"

I winced at the thought of what they might say or do, perhaps her dad would suddenly grow ten feet tall and have flames shooting out his ears as he would pick me up by the shoulders and say with a devilish demonic voice, "You did what to my daughter?"

I took a deep breath…and decided to wait for the right time to tell them.

Jen's morning sickness was more like day sickness, as she was nauseous all day long. It wasn't long before her mom was suspicious of her running to the bathroom every five minutes, especially when commercials for crunchy tacos would come on the TV.

Finally, Jen's mom, Julie, confronted her at their house, "Jen, what's wrong? You've been acting strange."

Jen looked at her mom and said, "I'm pregnant..."

Now, I wasn't there but, being the loving parents that they were, they hugged her and were actually excited, even more so when Jen told them we were getting married.

The next day when I came over, her parents sat us down in the living room. I was swimming in my skin with uneasiness as Tom looked at me and said, "Well. We hear you're going to be apart of the family."

A sigh of relief seeped from my soul. Tom and Julie were loving and accepting, nothing like the fiery tormenting confrontation that I had expected.

In November Jen and I were driving around town when she asked me if I wanted to see the house she grew up in.

"My parents have been renting it out to the tenants for the past seven years," she told me as we pulled into the cul-de-sac and saw the two story suburban home.

"It'd be awesome to live here if they rented it to us," I said, impressed with the cozy cul-de-sac of nice homes. We were going to be married in February, but we still hadn't found a place to live.

"Yeah it would, but I don't think they're planning on moving." She said with fond eyes looking at the front yard in which she used to play.

I **stare**d at the house and imagined all the wonderful times she had in the house, and thought it would be amazing to raise our family there too.

Then I held her hand and said, "Well, you never know what will happen when you pray about it." And so we prayed.

A week later, the tenants called up her parents and said that they had found a house that they were going to buy, and that they would be moving out at the end of December.

Jen called me up excited and told me the news, and all I could do was look up and thank God for the answered prayer.

I moved into the house on January 1st with my friend Cook 'em up Chris. Chris was a chef in training, which was great since Jen and I only knew how to make Top Ramen noodles and macaroni cheese.

During December and through January, I tried selling radio ads for a local radio station, but that fell through. I thought I was a good salesman, but they wanted quantity, not quality, so I found myself back at the restaurant slinging dishes.

Jen's mom Julie, began coming over to the house and started remodeling it, putting up fresh paint and new floors and carpet. I couldn't help but feel overwhelmed with how blessed my life had now become. Just a few years before, I was sleeping on people's couches with hangovers and smoky lungs, and now, my life was becoming stable. My move to Temecula was one of those life altering decisions that was becoming eternal…

Now it's February 12th and I'm standing in front of the romantically lit dining hall at Temeku Hills Country Club with all my friends and family facing me. My pastor is standing on stage waiting for the wedding party to join him.

There goes Moser in a tux with Jen's best friend Taylor in a royal blue dress walking past me.

Moser walks by and smirks.

I shrug my shoulders.

One by one, the wedding party steps onto the stage, and then suddenly a hush falls upon the crowd of 170 wedding guests.

And now, everyone's eyes turn to the back door, and as Shania Twain's song *From This Moment,* softly began playing over the speakers, the doors part. My heart falls and my eyes moisten as I see my bride, my beauty, the completion of my soul.

Her dad has his left arm latched with hers. He's wearing a tuxedo, with his white combed hair and smart looking glasses above his trademark mustache. I mention this because I doubt anyone is looking at him, because all eyes are on the most beautiful bride in the world.

Jen, her hair curled up ever so softly and sweetly, is walking towards me with a smile and a sensual **stare**. Her make up is beautiful, almost angelic, as gold glitter glistens her gorgeous body.

Tom and Jen stop and stand a few feet in front of me, then I hear Pastor Shawn's voice say, "Who brings forth this woman to be joined to this man?"

Tom smiles and smirks, somewhat funny, yet somewhat sadly, as he says, "Her mother and I."

Then he leans over and kisses his little girl ever so delicately. He shakes my hand and presents his beautiful daughter's soft sweet hand into mine.

The rest of the wedding becomes a blur…I remember standing on stage staring into Jen's eyes, hoping that we don't stutter our vows. Pastor Shawn, thin with blue eyes and a brown goatee, smiles and announces us Man and Wife. From this moment my life has meaning beyond all measure…my life has a passionate purpose…my life has become complete…well, except for one more thing…

Four months later Jen and I are in the Rancho Springs delivery room with Julie and Dr. Glaser.

"Push!" I say as I count one to ten in a slow methodical voice.

Jen's eyes glare at me like I'm an idiot; "I AM PUSHING!"

The doctor is staring between Jen's legs as he chomps casually on chewing gum, "I see the head, just one more long push and baby Jack should be here!"

One...Two...Push...

Three...Four...Push...

Five...Six...Push...

Seven...Eight...Push...

Nine...Ten...PUSH!!!

"Wha! Wha! Wha!" Our little baby Jack is screaming.

The doctor slaps him and wipes him off, then places him onto Jen's chest.

Jen's mom sighs, "Ahh, he's so beautiful."

Jen is crying as she looks at him and says, "I love you."

And me?

Well, people often ask what I thought about when Jack was born.

Honestly?

I didn't think of anything.

I was just completely blown away by the miracle of birth...and by God...and how everything in life, truly does *happen for a reason.*

Jen and I held Jack and looked into his eyes as he **stare**d curiously back into ours, then Jen and I **stare**d into each others eyes and smiled. Now, our life is complete.

CHAPTER
FORTY TWO

(Son Jack, 2 years old…)

"The routine of a normal life…"

Almost a year later, Jack is standing in his crib snarling at me. It's eight in the morning and I want to sleep for another hour or two…but that's not going to happen.

Not only can Jack snarl at me with a wrinkled nose and curled lip, but he can also wake Jen and I up with an intense whining cry that says, "Okay! Everybody UP!"

I pick Jack up from the crib, letting Jen sleep in, and take him downstairs as he says things that melt my heart, things like, "DAA, DAA, DAA, DAA," and when he knows he's getting a bottle, "Baa, Baa, Baa, Baa…"

Taking him into the kitchen I make him a bottle and hand it to him.

He snatches it away and sucks it down immediately.

I make Jen and me some coffee, and then **stare** at Jack as the coffee percolates. I laugh because this routine has become my life.

A few years earlier, at this time in the morning, I was either hanging over a toilet throwing up, or was sleeping on a stranger's couch with a head full of acid watching the walls melt into funny faces.

Now, the funny faces I see come from my son. As Jack finishes the bottle, he holds it up above his head and lets out a satisfied, "Ahhhh!" Then he drops the bottle behind him, and begins to crawl off into the living room.

I pour myself some coffee and follow him.

In our living room we have creatively constructed our couches in a certain formation that purposely cages Jack in. We have our couches, which are actually the same color, in an L shape around the television leaving two exits on either side. I put up a baby gate on one side, and then move a dining room chair to the other.

Jack squeals and snarls as he sees me do this as if to say, "Hey! I have places to go!"

I turn on a recorded version of Teletubbies and he claps his hands.

Jack likes Teletubbies because they bounce around and do cute things.

I like Teletubbies because it brings back memories of Brady and Adam doing acid and watching Teletubbies thinking that they actually were the characters on the show.

I think of Adam and miss him. Adam died just about four years ago, and his son, Nolan, would be four in just a few months.

Looking at my son Jack playing with his toys, I swell up with appreciation that I have the chance to spend time with him and hold him and hug him, unlike Adam. He died six months before his son was ever born…he never had the chance to look into his son's eyes.

But I can. I look into Jack's brown eyes, and see a little mini-me running around.

I think of Brady and how he had a son too. His son is almost three. Brady no longer did drugs either…he had now become a talented helmet designer.

Reflecting on our paths of life, the three of us, Brady, Adam and myself, I smile with sadness.

Brady made it…

I made it…

But Adam didn't.

Jack wobbles over to me and hands me some lint from the carpet. He smiles a toothless smile and says, "Daa Daa?"

"Thanks buddy, is this for me?"

He then **stare**s behind me and points, "Maa Maa…"

I turn to look and there is my beautiful wife. She is swiping the sleep from her eyes as she descends down the stairs.

"Did you make coffee?"

"Don't I always make coffee?"

Jack smiles until Jen passes him by on her way to the coffee machine, then he begins squealing and screaming and slapping the couch.

I glare at him, "Oh boo whoo."

He glares at me making fun of him, and his lip pouts out even further.

To instigate his frustrations even further, I toss a pillow at his head which makes him tip over.

He grunts and looks back up at me like I'm an ass.

Jen comes in blowing on her creamed coffee.

"Hiiiiii baby!" She says sweetly.

"Hi," I say.

"Not you...I was talking to Jack."

"What about me? Your extremely attractive husband that made you coffee?" I spout sarcastically.

And my wife, although she is so sweet and kind, but is also as much of a smart ass as I am, says, "My husband? Oh, he's here?"

I then make a flustered face and in a teasing voice, "Eww, you're so funny...did you stay up late watching Jay Leno, writing down your jokes? Because really, that was funny...No seriously. It was soooo funny. Look at me, I'm laughing because it was so funny."

She nods her head and pays attention to Jack. Then together as a family, we hang out and watch Family Guy the cartoon and add to our arsenal of sarcasm.

We laugh and tease each other, because we love each other and this is what we do.

Yes, we do this everyday.

I went from surviving like a rat in a sewer, to living like a normal family guy. I thought about how crazy life was and how it always changed.

Throughout our day, we'd take turns watching Jack. When she wanted to take a shower, I'd watch him. When I wanted to write, she'd watch him. The pace of life seemed to slow down from a few years ago when I used to watch for cops through my blinds and worry about the police busting in and arresting me for being on drugs.

But it had all changed.

Instead of living with random roommates, everyone from drug dealers to losers, I now lived with my witty wife and snarling son.

I have been blessed. Yes, I have been blessed.

CHAPTER
FORTY THREE

"Relay For Life..."

As the diapers piled up and baby cries kept the neighbors awake, the months went by and Jack got bigger by the day.

I got a job at the Red Lobster and started serving salads and shrimp again. My book had become stale and I was tired of looking at it and reading it for the millionth time. Although I was tired of reading it, there was still that nagging voice in my soul that said, *"It will happen."*

In April I got a call from JD's mom Genevive. Her voice was excited and eager to tell me that she had gotten a job at a promotions company that was putting on the Cancer Society's Relay For Life.

"John! You have to have your book ready to go!" She said almost like a commanding cheerleader.

"What? Why?"

"John, this event gets thousands of people that walk for 24 hours around the Cal State track and they raise money…you can have a booth out there and promote your book!" She nearly shouted.

"Umm, it's not done."

"Well get it done!"

The only problem was the event was less than a month away and she told me I had to raise $1,000 within the next 48 hours to meet the deadline.

On top of raising the $1,000 I also had to figure out someway of getting my book edited and published in about three and a half weeks.

But I figured if it was meant to happen, then it would….

I began calling up people for financial support and thankfully had a handful of people chip in for the thousand dollars.

Next and by far the biggest obstacle was the book itself. Having wrestled with the writing for the past five years, my head had become cloudy of the direction of the book and where to take it. I needed to see it with fresh eyes but couldn't find an editor or even a highly educated geek to sit down and get the job done.

That is, until Linda called.

Linda was my mother in-law's close friend and she actually organized my wedding for me. She was an extremely articulate person that had an exact agenda for every conversation, logical and strategic in every sense of being expedient.

"John, Julie tells me that you are looking for someone to edit your book, is this correct in my understanding?"

I smiled with the phone near my mouth, "Yes Linda. That is correct to your understanding."

Her voice became more directive, "Well listen. My friend Michael has written a variety of books and has the experience of being an editor as well. I would like to put you in contact with Michael so he can hopefully expedite the editing process."

"Great," I said with a laugh. "I like expedited editing."

She then gave me the number and I gave Michael a call in which he said he would be happy to do it.

A few weeks later I got the edited material back for my book, which I had decided to do the first 16 chapters as a symbolic way of introducing the book.

I was 16 when my mom died.

The book itself would be 38 chapters in full, as in the age she was when she passed.

With the editing done and just a few days left before the big event, I needed to figure out how the hell I was going to find somebody to print it up.

Seeing how Linda was so well connected in the town of Temecula where I lived, I needed her to be here and hoped that she would use her connections to make things happen. The only problem was she lived in Las Vegas…but its interesting how *Everything Happens for a Reason…*

The next day I got a call from my mother in law saying that Linda's car had broken down on her way through Temecula as she was on route to see her family a few towns away.

"Could you pick Linda up from the auto shop?"

I smiled as I began to see how the pieces were falling into place, "You bet I can."

Racing over to the auto shop I picked up the professional Linda and said, "Interesting how you break down in Temecula with the book event just a week away, huh?"

She laughed at the obvious coincidence, "Yeah…I think God has a plan."

Over the next few days Linda and I went to Copies N More and got 100 books printed up with an awesome looking red cover that Michael had designed. Not only did we get books for an excellent price, about $2 each, Linda also got an "In-Kind" sponsorship for T-shirts from her friend Dawn at BAM Promotional products.

When I got the first 100 books I couldn't help but start selling them all though I was going to need them for the event coming up. I went to the Red Lobster and announced that their lucky day had come. The servers and managers all looked at me like table monkeys without bananas, "What are you talking about?"

"My book is finally done!" I said holding a few dozen red covered books with *The Stare* designed on it.

A few hours later, I had sold almost half of the 100 books.

Word got out and people were coming up and buying a copy for themselves and their grandma's neighbor. The excitement continued to build as I ordered another 100 books for the event.

The morning we were going to leave for Bakersfield for the Relay for Life, my in-laws had rented an RV for the trip. So, Linda, myself, Jen and baby Jack along with Tom and Julie, we all packed into the motor home and made my book debut/return to Bakersfield. A dream unlike any other dream come true.

At the event we set up a tent and table with banners and books. Friends over the years came by and bought books and met my wife and Jack.

My step dad Dave and my sister Danielle came up to me and hugged me to show their support. I looked into Dave's eyes, and throughout the turbulent times of years past, he said what I had been longing to hear, "Well John, your mom would be proud of you...and...I'm proud of you, too."

That was a moment that I will never forget.

Moser made his way out there later that night, with his flask of whisky and head full of philosophies and we sat there between midnight and four in the morning talking like the old days.

"You know John," he said as if some ancient wise mystic, "All the things we used to talk about back at the apartment have come to pass."

I nodded.

"Look at you. Look where you're at in life. We prayed for strength and wisdom and look, three years later, you're sitting at your first book event with a beautiful wife and son, with in-laws that love and respect you."

I nodded. This is usually how it went…He'd talk and I'd nod.

"You know how many men throughout the ages that have strived for everything you have right now?"

I smiled, "I know."

He burped and took another swig from his flask.

"All the things that you didn't have…you now have."

"Like what?" I asked, prodding him to go further.

"I remember when we lived together and my mom and dad would come over with my brothers and my sister, and you looked so lonely. You didn't have that traditional sense of family after your mom died. But now," he pointed exaggeratedly around us, "Now, you have it all. You're releasing your book at the Cancer event in Bakersfield…don't you see how many different ways that's symbolic?"

I shrugged my shoulders.

"You've returned home from your voyage to the far off land of Temecula, with your wife and son and your book, to a place where you once went to school for what, like, two weeks, at a Cancer event. That's powerful."

He smirked as did I.

"But best of all, John," he said leaning in, putting his hand on my shoulder and drunkenly declaring, "You have your friend, big-bad-wild-turkey-whiskey-drinking-Moser!"

We both laughed.

"I love you John," he said being serious, "You make me proud and you inspire me."

I shrugged sarcastically, "Yeah, well, I *am* the coolest guy you know…"

We laughed again.

As we walked across the grass to his car where his girlfriend was waiting for him, amongst the darkest part of the night with the overhead stadium lights shining down like a radiant pale ghost, I thought in my mind how this journey was now coming to an end within itself. The struggles over the past few years had seemed to let up a bit. The storm of life had calmed, and the peaceful waters of destiny seemed to be flowing like a river. All the reasons and questions seemed to be answered, and the ones that hadn't been, one day would.

We got to his car and he turned to me and said, "You know your mom would be proud, right?"

I shrugged and nodded my head, "I hope so."

"John," he squeezed my shoulder, "You know so. You've made her immortal in a sense. All these people that read this story and read about your mom…that makes her immortal. She is now alive within so many people's minds…out of her death, you have given her life. She'd be proud."

I smiled.

He smirked.

Then we gave each other a hug and went our separate ways, into the night, and into the light of our own new journeys.

I knew my mom would be proud. I just couldn't wait to see her again…

CHAPTER
FORTY FOUR

"The Circle of Life…"

With sweaty hands I shut off my motorcycle. A summer sunset projected long shadows across the Mesa Marin foothills.

My dirt bike growled to a stop as I parked alongside a tree next to my mom's grave and I quietly enjoyed the peaceful panoramic view of so many lives lived.

A cloud of dust settled over the cemetery I had just ridden through and the silence from my ceased motor saturated the souls of the cemetery.

"It's hot," I uttered to myself, my words like vapors. I rested my elbows on the handlebars and took in a deep breath. To my right I could see tombstones stitched across acres of green grass, to my left was a stone colored square that covered my mother's grave.

I leaned my dirt bike next to the tree, and walked over to her tombstone and read it like I had done so many times in the past seven years:

"Karen Lynn Donnelly...beloved wife and mother...January 14, 1960-June 5, 1998."

Again, I took another deep breath. My voice captured by the moment, staring at the grave in the ground.

"Hi mom," I said softly, the words floating from my mouth onto her grave.

A soft wind blew through the blades of grass and across my face. I looked to the west and saw the sun setting amongst soft swirling clouds.

I fell to my knees and placed both of my hands on top of her tombstone, and then I knelt down closer and kissed it.

"Well mom, I'm a dad and a husband now," I chuckled, imagining her laughing and smiling. A tear ran down my face. I closed my eyes and sensed deep within myself that she was sitting there next to me.

"I got something for you," I said, reaching into a backpack and pulling out my manuscript.

"You always joked that I'd grow up and write a book someday, and well, I guess you were right."

I put the thick white file of papers on her grave. Another tear ran down my cheek, but I swiped it away.

"Thought you might want to read it, you know, make sure there aren't any typos or anything," I joked.

The edges of the paper pulled up and wavered with the wind, almost as if she were thumbing through it.

In my heart I heard the soft sweetness of her loving laugh.

I reached into the backpack again, and pulled out a picture of her new grandson. "Here you go mom, a picture of little baby Jack. Cute, huh?" I laid his picture next to the manuscript and **stare**d at it.

"Amazing how it all worked out, eh?"

Again, I could sense that she was laughing.

I sat there and watched the movie screen of my mind replay the past eight years. I remember sitting next to her grave as a sixteen year old staring at her casket, incapable of comprehending her death. My thoughts traveled back through the troubled years of drugs and alcohol, and how I was trying to kill myself, thinking that I'd be one step closer to my mom through death. The instability of moving more than twenty times, the chaos of all the choices that I had made, and now, at twenty four, how I was stable and married with a wonderful wife and a sweet son.

"I can't believe I survived," I said out loud with a laugh.

Then I rolled over and sat down next to her grave placing my elbows on my knees, staring out over the grass and across the road to a tall spiky palm tree where Adam Pierce was buried. There had been so much death in the past eight years, but now, it had blossomed into so much life, and promise and hope.

I smiled and sighed, "Well, I guess everything *does happen for a reason!*"

A few birds flew across the sky and disappeared into hope's horizon.

Above Adam's palm tree, the massive orange sun melted into the scenic background mountains of Western Bakersfield.

As it faded into the promise of a new tomorrow, I **stare**d at it somewhat sadly, knowing deep within myself that one long story of my life had come to a close. Yet, with tomorrow, another one would soon begin.

And with that peaceful thought inside my mind, I laid down on my back atop my mother's grave and with all the other souls in the cemetery I **stare**d up at the eternal heavens above…and thought of God and of angels and of all the wonderful majestic things to come.

What was once the beginning had become the end.

And with the end, would come another beginning.

Indeed, this life is ever changing.

Tomorrow will always be different; today will always seem the same…and yesterday will always seem like a lost memory.

And what will be left, is *the stare* of our lives in our eyes.

THE END

What happened to???

In order of appearance…

Jared: Last I heard Jared had a baby and was marrying an older woman who had 4 kids of her own. I lost contact with him a few years ago and am trying to locate him.

Step Dad Dave: My step dad Dave met a woman two years later, got married in a drive thru wedding chapel on his Harley in Vegas, and then got a divorce a few years later. He is starting life over with new enthusiasm, and our relationship has been reestablished better than ever. He enjoys being Jack's grandpa.

Danielle: After our mom's death, Danielle turned inward and became a book worm. She ended up graduating high school with straight A's, and was accepted to UCSD and after a year there, she transferred to Tulane University in Louisiana.

Mom: My mom would have celebrated her 47th birthday on January 14th, 2007 (which was the day Danielle left for Louisiana…symbolic, eh?). As far as I know she is probably up in heaven laughing at us.

Aunt Patty: My aunt Patty owns a dental office in Glendora. She adopted a baby girl from China, Jenny, to be the sister of her oldest daughter Julie.

Brady: Brady became a professional helmet designer who is married with two kids and lives in Bakersfield.

Brett: *As far as I know, Brett still owns a business in Bakersfield and lives with his four kids and wife with a dirt bike track in his backyard.*

Mr. Wells: *Wesley Wells is now the principal at a high school in Bakersfield.*

Justin Roberts: *Justin Roberts married his high school sweet heart where they both graduated from college in San Deigo.*

Daniel: *Daniel got married but I heard they split up and he ended up joining the marines.*

Jerry (JD) McCaslin: *After CMX, JD ended up getting hurt and stopped riding. He has a daughter and is trying to get his life in order.*

My Dad John III: *My dad went on to start several successful automotive internet companies and married Jessie. They had a little girl named Jade in April 2004 (so I have a sister 23 years younger than me). They invest in real estate and split their time between Malibu and New Zealand.*

Ray Crumb: *Ray closed his clothing shop a few years later (hopefully not because of the sickly sandwiches...) and he is a professional test rider for Honda.*

Adam Pierce: *Adam was killed in a car accident on June 22, 2002. He left behind a son who was born six months later named Nolan Adam Samuel Pierce. From what I hear, Nolan is a spitting image of his father, and already at the age of four, is tearing up the dirt on a little motorcycle.*

Gafford: Gafford had a son as well, but at this time Gafford is considered missing in action. Nobody seems to know what happened to him. I thought of making milk cartons with his picture on it, but haven't gotten around to it as of yet.

Brian Ferrell: Brian moved out of the house and got married.

Drunk Todd: He's drunk.

Bob: Bob is still Bob. He still wears his Bob belt buckle and goes to Jake's Tex Mex at least three times a week and orders half a chicken sandwich, chocolate chip cookie and ice tea, while he mentors young people. He's as solid and consistent as can be.

Jason: After breaking both of his feet in a dirt bike accident, Jason made a radical change of life, going from an alcoholic drug addict, to full fledged soldier for Christ. He is heavily involved with church and inspires many of the people he used to party with. He also got certified to become a respiratory therapist and works at various hospitals.

Tyson: Tyson still lives in Bakersfield, although the skate shop closed down shortly after I left Bakersfield.

Tyler Durden: Tyler joined several bands, but none of them came together. He is still the most talented person I know. He sang a solo of "Simple Kind of Man" at my wedding.

Bruce: Bruce can still be found on the street corners late at night, usually drunk, singing for money in his guitar case.

Beth: Beth got married and moved to Utah and had a beautiful daughter. She then moved back to California.

Craig: Craig became very successful in his carpentry business and now owns a boat which he sails around the Long Beach Harbor.

Jackson: Jackson still works for Craig, "You know what I'm sayin' huh?"

Moser: Moser had a son named Hunter (named after his favorite author Hunter S. Thompson) on January 13, 2007. He works as a carpenter and is getting married this fall. He is still my writing mentor, philosophical counselor and best friend.

Aunt Mary and Uncle Dick: They are retired and still live in Braintree Massachusetts, where they enjoy their grandkids. Mary is heavily involved with her church as a spiritual mentor.

Nana and Red: Nana goes to church every morning at 7 o'clock while Red goes golfing. We live a mile away from them.

Jen and Jack: Jen gets to stay at home with Jack while he terrorizes our cat and destroys our house. They both get to put up with me. We are expecting our second son October 2007.

Chef Chris: Got married and had a son.

Linda: Linda fell in love with a man and moved to New Mexico where she works with various non-profit organizations where she expedites things.

Michael Wells: Michael is extremely busy with several creative projects, everything from writing, to editing, to web designing, to a multi-level Arbonne Business. He is extremely talented and helps me produce things when he has the time. He can be reached at Michael@nighthawk7.com

My In-laws: They say you don't just marry the person, you marry your in-laws too. Well for me, that worked out great, because my in-laws are my best friends. I talk to my mother-in-law at least everyday, and my father-in-law formats my books for me. They are the most supportive people I know. My idea of a good time is hanging out at their house and hitting golf balls from their front yard into the orchards across the street, or sitting on their patio with my father-in-law while reading books or barbequing.

As for me: I'm still writing…

SPECIAL THANKS...

They say that writing is a lonely venture...but getting to the point of publishing sure isn't. I wouldn't be where I am today without the help of the following people that came along at just the right time during my writing journey, and gave me the courage to complete my mission.

Michael Wells and his efficient editing and graphic design. Wendi Rachel for her creative photography. Linda Murillo for her ability to expedite things. Dawn at BAM promotions for her kind sponsorships. Joe and Jay at Copies N More in Temecula for printing the pre-published copies of this book.

Sarah Peckham for her encouragement and promotional planning. Mary Poehner for her last minute revisions and editing.

Eric Moser for his drunken philosophies of life, death and writing.

Red Jacobsen for his witty puns and *pun*ctuation editing (Get it, Red? Oh, Pun!) To my Nana for all her prayers and support. John and Jessie Butler for their love, support, encouragement and sponsorship.

Bob Swanson for his fundamental faith, loving discipline and sound wisdom.

Tom Smith for his excellent layout and formatting skills, as well as paying for printer paper and cartridges and anything else that might've happened to my computer. Julie Smith for her encouragement, motherly love and support.

And to my wife...
Who always reminded me that rent was due
and that I needed to finish my book so I could pay it.

BOOK DISCUSSION GUIDE

1. Throughout The Stare, the author makes references to light, such as sunrises, sunsets and shadows. How does this make you feel about the emotion and overall tone of the book?

2. If you have lost somebody close to you, do you feel that the author clearly articulates the feelings associated with such a loss? Why or why not?

3. How would you describe the writing of The Stare?

4. During the author's numerous psychedelic episodes, do you think the writing accurately describes the experience?

5. Did The Stare affect you emotionally? How so?

6. What was your favorite part of The Stare?

7. Was there a part of the story that you felt the author could've written more about? If so, what was it?

8. As the author turned his life around spiritually, did you see this as a logical sequence considering the trials and tribulations that the author went through?

9. Do you agree that *Everything Happens for a Reason*? If so, what in your life has brought reason and meaning to it?

10. Did you find the book to be humorous? If so, what was the funniest part?

11. In the stories about Dickweed, did you think that the name was funny or offensive?

12. In your opinion, what was the turning point in the story which led from the dark side of life to a lighter side?

13. It seems that the author always tried to connect with his dead mother during psychedelic trips…in your opinion, why was this?

14. Based on the story, what do you think the author's personality is like?

15. Throughout the story, what character seems to be the most memorable? Why?

16. If you could ask the author anything, what would it be?

17. Do you believe in Heaven? If so, what do you think it is like?

18. What are your spiritual views? Do you agree or disagree with the author's Christian point of view? Why?

19. Did you think this book dealt more with cancer, death, drugs, spirituality or writing? How would you describe it to a friend?

20. If you could recommend this book to somebody, who would it be?

Contact the Author

John Butler is available for speaking, seminar and lecture events in regards to cancer, addiction, spirituality or writing.

Author is also available for book signing events as well as interviews.

Book clubs interested in a conference call with the author can contact him by e-mail.

If this book has impacted you in some way or if you would like to join the efforts in making this book successful, please write the author with your story or ideas.

The best way to contact the author is at:

jbutler835@yahoo.com

Shirts, stickers and other goodies available at...
www.johnbutlersbook.com
or
www.myspace.com/johnbutlersfanclub